REVENUE
GROWTH
PLATFORM

JAN ROPPONEN / SAMI LAMPINEN

REVENUE GROWTH PLATFORM - A strategic and tactical guidebook for securing growth

©Jan Ropponen & Sami Lampinen 2018

Graphics: Mikko Johansson

Contact publisher:
www.axend.fi
+358 50 5169392
jan.ropponen@axend.fi

ISBN 978-952-69079-1-8 (paperback)
ISBN 978-952-69079-2-5 (eBook)

TABLE OF CONTENTS

PART III

PUTTING THE RIGHT ROLES, PROCESSES AND TECHNOLOGY IN YOUR PLATFORM

INTRODUCTION

We used to live in a product-centric world, where companies operated in siloes and focused on efficiently distributing products to the market. This worked, and companies grew without really ever being connected to their customers. We are now moving into a world, where customers demand results and outcomes, not just products. At the same time, expectations towards companies have increased because the products and services that they provide are only one factor that customers take into consideration in their decision-making. According to a study, buyers are 5.2 times more likely to purchase from companies that provide a great customer experience.* This tells us that we now truly live in a customer-empowered world, where companies that are connected to their customers will survive and thrive.

Success in this new and demanding environment, requires that companies deliver high-quality customer engagement as predictably and efficiently as modern factories create products, without compromising on quality. Each part of the customer's journey from customer acquisition to account management must be orchestrated to perfection in a personalized fashion.

Many think that implementing technology is enough to solve inefficiencies and quality problems in customer management. Sure enough, without technology, building a modern organization that scales and grows is impossible, but at the same time technology on its own is not enough. A more holistic approach is needed to achieve growth.

Earlier, the solution for growing was to hire more salespeople and push more products to the market, and this way revenue would increase proportionally as the head count was increased. A sales organization was an army of individual artists that were given a territory and monitored so they achieved their quotas. Nowadays, the companies that are growing still have sales teams, but the role of an individual salesperson has been split up into many different roles. Sales has become a science, just like supply chain optimization. Many excellent sales books have been published in the past years, but the problem for someone who wants to develop an organization more holistically is that these books focus on a very specific sales methodology, not on how you can build an overall successful modern organizational operating model – process, roles, and technology included. Some books do focus on the organization more holistically, but they unfortunately often emphasize only new customer acquisition.

---

* media.dmnews.com/images/2013/09/23/cx_infographic_full_size_463272.png (Temkin Group)

The opportunities to modernize sales organizations are everywhere and some companies need a model or roadmap to follow. We decided to take a journey to piece together models and frameworks that companies can use to modernize their businesses. The starting points for companies can be radically different; both from the perspective of what the company sells and its stage of maturity. In software sales for example, many companies already have advanced go-to market models, whereas many traditional companies still operate sales and marketing in a very similar fashion to how they operated 30 years ago.

PLATFORM THINKING BECAME A CENTRAL PART OF THE BOOK

As we combined our findings with our practical experience from the field, we quickly realized that modern companies are succeeding because they are better at connecting with customers than their competitors are. Successful sales organizations are performing better than their competitors because of their leaner processes, which are scalable. They therefore do not only compete with the skills of their workforce, but with their processes and systems that allow their workforce to perform optimally every day. Companies that have winning processes, can recruit average sales people and make them perform at above average levels. This combination gives the capacity to consistently provide a great customer experience and scale predictably.

We call this 'Growth Platform thinking' and it is this that distinguishes the most successful organizations from their competitors. Growth Platform thinking is a way of developing a business in a holistic way that takes technology, processes, people, and products and services into consideration, and combines all of these elements to form one unified platform. In a Growth Platform, the customer and their lifecycle is at the center and the organization and technology is a platform that exists symbiotically, to enable the efficient steering of customers from one stage to the next in the relationship. The winners of tomorrow are built on this Growth Platform thinking.

WHO IS THIS BOOK WRITTEN FOR?

Revenue Growth Platform is for those who want to modernize their business, to achieve growth and a stronger competitive advantage. This book provides both strategic and tactical insights that you will be able to use in developing your business. Regardless of your background or experience, we are sure there are beneficial ideas for you spread out throughout the different chapters.

To give you a broad enough perspective, we have interviewed and studied both small startups and large mature companies to identify common best practices. Large companies can learn from smaller, more agile companies, and vice versa. Startups are building their business models from scratch and they are investing in scalable technology platforms right from the beginning. Startups focus on rapid growth, while larger, more established companies can benefit immensely by streamlining their way of working to increase profits. The size of your company is not necessarily a deciding factor in how much you will benefit from this book. It's more a question of the development phase in which your own sales, marketing and service functions are in. Among those interviewed were, for example, two employees from companies that Forbes listed in 2018 as among the top 100 most innovative companies. One of these was KONE and the other was Salesforce.[*]

After reading Revenue Growth Platform, we want you to be able to execute your business more predictably than ever before, as well as launch new products and services more efficiently. "Growth" and "scalability" are two words that repeat throughout this entire book. If you find these themes interesting, then you have the right book in your hands.

Enjoy Revenue Growth Platform and most importantly, do take action on the ideas and insights you will find. Let us know how it goes!

Jan Ropponen & Sami Lampinen
Helsinki, Finland

Ps.
If you enjoy what you read, please do give us a review on Amazon and if you want to mention the book on social media, please do so with the hashtag **#revgrowthplatform**

INTRODUCING THE INTERVIEWED COMPANIES AND EXPERTS

Throughout the book there are many different example cases, but also seven interviews with leading thinkers in their own field of expertise whom we personally interviewed. Many companies are doing fantastic things that should be benchmarked and applied across other industries. The interviews will not only inspire with their insight, but also make it easier to understand the core concepts of this book so that you can take action.

SURF AIR – HOW DO YOU TURN AROUND AND COMPLETELY REDEFINE AN OLD BUSINESS MODEL?

We wanted to understand how the mentality of a subscription business differs from that of a traditional business. What are the true difficulties of completely redefining the business model of an industry that has always worked the same way? How should marketing and sales change when shifting from single transactions to focusing on a continuous relationship? To get answers to these questions we interviewed Simon Talling-Smith, CEO of Surf Air Europe. Simon explains what it takes to unlearn the old business model in Chapter 3.

KONE – WHAT DO CUSTOMER EXPERIENCE AND STRATEGY HAVE TO DO WITH EACH OTHER?

KONE is a company that has consistently been able to grow year after year. Not only does KONE have a great track record of growth as a company, but they have lately also been attracting headlines about their innovations and development with talking elevators and predictive maintenance. KONE was ranked 59th in the world, and 7th most innovate in Europe on Forbes' most innovative companies list 2018. Their new strategy is 'Winning with Customers' and we wanted to find out how this strategy is translated into concrete actions. Mikko Leinonen, Head of Customer and Sales Solutions, gives us a breakdown of what the strategy means and how this translates to marketing and sales development initiatives.

SALESFORCE – HOW DOES A CUSTOMER SUCCESS PIONEER ACCOMPLISH CUSTOMER SUCCESS?

As companies shift their focus to recurring business models, the need to constantly create value has pushed many companies to create customer success organizations. We didn't just want to hear thoughts about customer success from any company, we wanted insights from a pioneer and Salesforce is widely considered a pioneer in customer success. Their ability to keep and grow customers is a big reason why they were the fastest enterprise software company to reach an annual revenue of $10 billion. We had the pleasure to interview Marco Clazing, Head of Customer Success in North Europe, to get a glimpse of how Salesforce thinks about customer success and how they are organized to be able to offer great customer success.

KIM METCALF-KUPRES – HOW TO COMBINE SALES AND MARKETING ON A STRATEGIC LEVEL?

Having been VP and Chief Marketing Officer of Johnson Controls from 2013–2017, Kim has had a bird's eye view of the sales and marketing operations of a multibillion-dollar global business. (Johnson Controls revenue was slightly over 30 billion USD in 2017.*) With Kim, we had the chance to walk through topics, such as: what have been the key changes in marketing and sales? What happens if marketing and sales are not aligned? What types of metrics should be used? A very interesting part of the interview with Kim is the discussion around the implementation of technology and how attitudes towards its adoption have changed in a more positive direction, while expectations of users have simultaneously grown. Another topic we cover in the interview with Kim is: how can leaders drive change in larger transformation projects, such as CRM and marketing automation implementations?

ZUORA – WHY SHOULD COMPANIES IMPLEMENT A SUBSCRIPTION MODEL AND HOW WILL SALES AND MARKETING NEED TO CHANGE?

Zuora provides software for companies to run their subscription businesses, so they have a great overview of how different companies are moving to the subscription model and what the best practices are. Zuora's CEO has even coined the term 'Subscription Economy', which describes business models in this new era, in contrast to the old product-centric economy. We had the pleasure to interview the General Manager of EMEA for Zuora, John Phillips, to hear about the Subscription Economy, which he advises companies "not to underestimate". John tells us what the drivers of the Subscription Economy are and why it makes financial sense for companies to take this very seriously. John shares his insights on the best practices of shifting to a subscription model and the pitfalls to avoid, what the new metrics are and how to use technology.

LEADFEEDER – HOW DO YOU GROW WITHOUT A TRADITIONAL B2B SALES ORGANIZATION?

Leadfeeder is a B2B technology company that offers a solution for marketing and sales professionals to better identify the companies visiting their website. They've built a very lean and efficient sales model, which they are scaling now. We interviewed the Chief Sales Officer Jaakko Paalanen. When Jaakko talks about Leadfeeders commercial organization, he talks about "The Sales machine". In his interview he walks us through the different roles and responsibilities of the people working in their sales machine. Traditionally sales leaders focus on getting deals to close, but Jaakko being a modern sales leader, also emphasizes the importance of onboarding and customer success.

SMARP – WHAT IS THE ROLE OF A MODERN MARKETING TEAM?

Smarp is a company that is a pioneer in employee advocacy, with a solution for employee knowledge sharing. Niklas Sluijter is the CMO of Smarp. Being a fast-growing technology company, there is a lot of pressure on Niklas's marketing team to perform at a high level. With Niklas we cover many topics, of which these are a few: how are the roles divided between sales and marketing, and how are goals and KPIs divided between them? How do marketing and sales cooperate? What is the role of technology and what are the new things to be excited about? Niklas also gives four pieces of advice for fellow marketing professionals, but the advice is actually highly relevant for anyone working in a company that wants to achieve growth quickly.

PART I

THE PRESSURES TO CHANGE

CHAPTER 1

/ THE TWO MAJOR PRESSURES

Many things around us are changing, and while many businesses struggle, many are successful because of their fast pace of innovation and ability to adapt to new customer needs. Out of the 500 companies on the Fortune 500 list in 1955, only 12% are on the same list today.[*]

Changes can be seen in today's business environment from an environmental, political, social, economic and technological perspective, but from a B2B perspective, however, there are two major changes that rise above others. These two major changes are i) how business models are changing, and ii) how customers have become empowered. These are the two major changes we focus on in the first part of the book, which is Chapters 1 to 4.

Neither of these two major changes has happened at the same time or at any specific time, but different industries have been impacted by the changes either slowly or rapidly. Now that the business environment is truly global and connected, new ideas that have the potential to disrupt markets are receiving funding faster than before, and this in turn is also increasing the speed at which business models are changing.

#1 – CHANGING BUSINESS MODELS

Customers now demand more flexibility and better results from their vendors, because they have so many options about whom to buy from, and are under pressure to make good decisions and get the most value out of their purchases. At the same time, the capabilities and technology that are available is making it possible to try out and launch new business models relatively easily.

Technology and the need to become more efficient in all areas of business, is leading to new business models.

In industrial products, such as jet engines, the business model was already very advanced 50 years ago e.g. Rolls-Royce's 'Power by the hour' concept (see more about Rolls-Royce in Chapter 2). Technology, like IoT and other connected systems, is making it possible to bundle and build software and services around products. For example, Caterpillar, the construction manufacturing company, has launched CAT© Connect Solutions which enables customers to track, monitor and analyze how their machines are working in order to improve their onsite efficiency.[*] This change is what many call 'servitization'. Servitization is really a fundamental change because it moves manufacturers away from selling products in a transactional manner, to partnering with customers by providing services or capabilities around

[*] Ten Tzuo, *Subscribed*, p. 12.
[*] www.cat.com/en_US/by-industry/construction/cat-connect.html

the products. The customer is at the center, and the solutions are built around their needs. New companies that are changing old business models and making asset-sharing more efficient are for example Airbnb and Uber. Even Apple has gone through a business transformation. They used to provide stand-alone computer products, and now they have a whole ecosystem of products, along with iTunes, the App Store and iCloud, as examples of services in the ecosystem. Software companies are now in the cloud, offering software-as-a-service, or subscriptions instead of one-time fees. One thing that all these examples have in common is that we don't live in a product-centric world any longer. Products have become commoditized and companies can no longer only compete on traditional products.

Another big change in business models centers on the power to control the relationship with the customer. The companies that are the most proficient at being in touch and connected with customers are the most profitable, and they have an ability to increase their total addressable market by offering customers additional services and products, because they control the relationship and have the most knowledge about these customers. Business model change is about companies creating more value for customers. The companies that are closest to their customers and most willing to change will reap the benefits in growth and profits. Therefore, business model

transformation is more important than ever and many executives are taking note.

In a Forbes Insights study[*], which surveyed 400 top global executives,

70% of survey respondents were "extremely concerned" or "somewhat concerned" about whether their company would still be relevant and competitive in two years.

#2 – CUSTOMERS ARE EMPOWERED

Traditionally, buyers had to rely on sales people and advertising for information about products before making a purchasing decision. In those days, the seller had the power, because they held the information, but now the power has shifted to the buyer, thanks to the internet. Buyers can do their research independently and compare options in an unprecedented fashion. With a quick Google search the buyer has the world at their fingertips. This shift in power from seller to buyer, is described by Forrester as the 'Age of the Customer'. This shift puts huge emphasis on the experience the customer has when buying and using the products they have bought, and this means that marketing, sales and service must create more value than before. Mass marketing and generic customer service is not enough to create the type of customer experience that is needed to differentiate from competitors and retain happy customers. Companies must create the capabilities and culture to build and nurture personal relationships with customers. In our interview with Mikko Leinonen of KONE, he describes where marketing is heading with these words: "instead of working with large segments, we can pretty soon personalize all communications and interactions with customers, no matter which channel we are communicating through or which employee is talking to the customer." You'll find this interview in Chapter 4.

In the future, companies will not be able to market effectively to customers who haven't given them permission to do so. This was the main concept of visionary Seth Godin's book Permission Marketing, written already in 1999. The point is that a company must get a customer's consent to be able to communicate with them. It is now more relevant than ever that sellers create value and a great customer experience to enable them to get permission from customers. This is a major shift in marketing, but sales is also experiencing a change as the sales role changes. Customers are equipped with so much information that the sales

representative's role must also become more consultative. This is especially true for example in the automobile industry, where customers can do extensive research before going to a dealership.

For this reason, BMW introduced their Genius concept.[*] Instead of having a traditional sales person in the dealership, BMW has a BMW Genius who is a customer service person and highly trained to educate customers. When a customer arrives at the dealership they are assisted with all their questions and the BMW Genius remains available even after their purchase of a vehicle. This is a B2C example, but in B2B we have seen exactly the same shift take place as the role of the sales executive is transforming from a product-oriented sales role, to a more consultative or advisory role.

WHERE THESE TWO CHANGES LEAD US

These two major changes explained in this chapter put pressure on companies to operate in a more customer-centric fashion. This means shifting focus to the whole lifecycle of the customer relationship, instead of operating according to a transactional relationship mindset. Shifting the business model from products to services means the commercial organization must change, and that is something we will look at in more detail in Chapters 5 to 10. In those chapters we will focus

* Read more here about BMW Genius at the website of BMW www.bmw.ca/en/topics/experience/Genius.html

more on the tactical aspect of building a success-ful modern commercial organization.

New business models and the empowered customer are two intertwined forces, that cannot only be met with changes in sales, marketing and service, but also the offering itself must change to become more customer-centric and that is what the next chapter is about.

#1 BUSINESS MODEL CHANGE

- Customers want outcomes, not products

- Subscriptions give flexibility

- Instead of ownership, customers want value

Products become services that create continuous value for customers

#2 CUSTOMERS ARE EMPOWERED

- Ease of comparing products and making smart choices

- Wealth of information available 24/7

- Global access to goods and services

- Highly independent customers

Sales, marketing and service create value for customers in all stages of the customers lifecycle

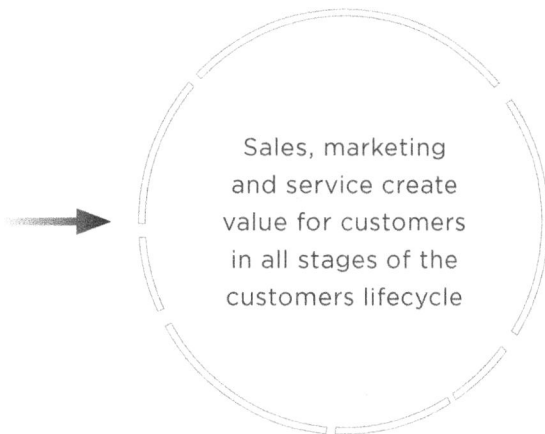

CUSTOMER EXPERIENCE becomes the competitive advantage

CHAPTER 2

/ CUSTOMERS WANT OUTCOMES

There are numerous ways that customers can benefit more these days from products and services, which leads us to a major topic that needs to be highlighted which is the subscription business model. To find the root of the subscription business model you need to go back about 500 years. In those days, exploration and map documentation was financed through a subscription model. Those who paid a subscription fee received updated maps as explorers traveled the globe and made more finds.[*] Then magazine and newspaper publishers adopted this model in Europe in the 17th century. The subscription business model, therefore, isn't exactly anything new, but what is new and exciting is that the subscription business model can be applied to nearly any business.

When combining the trend for subscriptions with the power of digitalization, you can see that the opportunity is there not only for media and digital products, but also even low-ticket items and expensive industrial machines. Everything could potentially become subscription-based or, as we will examine later in this part, outcome-based. Digitalization is certainly providing lots of opportunities to make a lot of things available by subscription, not just low-cost products. Elevators, and other capital-heavy expenditure investments, are lower-margin products, while servicing the products remain a high-margin activity. Combining products and servicing, and charging either by usage or a time-bound fee is the business model shift that is either already a reality in many industries, or the future for industries that haven't yet changed. Additionally, all these products can be enhanced and connected digitally. Even cheap products can now have preventive maintenance contracts, because the cost of tracking and monitoring has decreased.

Whether making money from servicing products or enabling customers to subscribe, there is plenty of evidence that we are moving in the direction of outcomes, not products. Some describe this shift to outcomes in the manufacturing industry simply with the term servitization. In this chapter, we'll look at some different points of view on how customers are benefitting from subscriptions and what other possibilities exist to bundle value for customers, instead of just selling products. But first let's examine what is causing the change and how companies are taking advantage of the new capabilities that technology has provided.

SOFTWARE IS MAKING THE WORLD INTELLIGENT

With the cloud, analytics, IoT capabilities and massive leaps in computing power it has become possible to track even the use of cheaper products and have full visibility 24/7. Everything that can

[*] John Warrillow, *The Automatic customer – Creating a subscription business in any industry*

become digital and create value for customers, will become digital. The whole world is becoming leaner through digitalization. Consumers and companies are not so fixated on owning things, but are instead making sure they pay for what they are using in an optimal way.

Marc Andreessen, quoted in the Wall Street journal, said that "software is eating the world". Software and technology in general is making the world leaner and more intelligent by replacing or enhancing physical goods that we have had before. Imagine everything that is possible with applications on your mobile device: camera, notebook, wallet, thermometer, watch, music player, books, magazines and news, recorder, reminders/ To do lists, calendar, calculator, game console, TV remote, maps, email, just to name a few. Software is not only replacing physical products, it is also enhancing the physical world. Heavy machinery has IoT capabilities and it can be programed and tracked. There are so many problems and costs that can now be solved with IoT systems. For example, in the car manufacturing industry, stoppages in the production process cost on average 22,000 USD per minute. That's 1.3 million USD per hour.[*] IoT systems can help avoid unnecessary stoppages in production facilities and ensure elevators and escalators are always working in busy buildings. But it is not just for more expensive equipment that this applies, it's also for cheaper items, like toothbrushes. Oral-B's toothbrush comes equipped with a Bluetooth connection[**] so users can track if they are brushing their teeth often enough and in the right way.

IoT and applications can be used to monitor and control machinery, doors, any tools and now with artificial intelligence we will see a great deal of traditionally manual and error-prone labor become automated.

PRODUCTS AND SERVICES FLOW SMOOTHLY IN THE DIGITAL AGE

Not only has technology made the exchange of products from one owner to the next much easier; products are now also shared more smoothly between owners of assets and users. The ease of access to products and transparency about where to buy goods and services and for how much is creating a smoother balance of demand and supply, which is benefiting buyers as prices decrease.

Logistics is becoming easier as new technology helps orchestrate the logistics chain. This has led to sharing of not just cheaper products but also more expensive items like cars, homes and heavy machinery. Physical goods, software and services are being packaged and delivered continuously in a more flexible fashion and scaled so that everyone using a certain product can benefit. Sharing physical products is becoming easier, which means that unless a B2B company contin-

[*] iiot-world.com/connected-industry/the-cost-of-one-minute-downtime-in-manufacturing/
[**] beta.techcrunch.com/2015/02/17/oral-b-pro-7000-smartseries-with-bluetooth-review/

uously needs machinery for products, or needs a fleet of trucks or cars, then there are going to be more flexible options than the traditional leasing model. People and companies are subscribing to more and more products and services because of the increase in digital products/software and the increase of physical products that have become enhanced by software in some way. In this chapter we will examine some different ways companies are providing customers with flexible and connected solutions.

PAY AS YOU GO

Paying as you use a product is often connected to Rolls-Royce's trademarked concept, 'Power by the hour', which was introduced in 1962 when Rolls-Royce Viper engines were offered as 'Power by the hour'. This meant that customers paid for the hours they used the engines, while Rolls-Royce took responsibility for replacing parts and taking care of maintenance.[*]

Today, through its TotalCare® service, Rolls-Royce allows customers to lock in a fixed cost for operating a Rolls-Royce engine. Rolls-Royce takes full care of everything related to operational support, repair and overhaul, as well as information management, thereby helping customers maximize the flying potential of their engines.[**]

This means Rolls-Royce is fully aligned with customers, and the cost of ownership is predictable for the customer.

Customers mitigate the risks associated with ownership because they are guaranteed an engine and replacement service. Rolls-Royce has been able to provide this service by having real-time performance using onboard sensors that can alert engineers around the world and pinpoint problems even before an aircraft has landed. If problems occur, they also have a global network of authorized maintenance centers that can help with unscheduled maintenance, thereby removing the risk for customers of unpredictable and costly maintenance.[***]

The same approach that Rolls-Royce has taken can be applied to nearly anything that requires maintenance.

SUBSCRIPTIONS

A pioneer in subscriptions in the software industry[****] is Salesforce. Thanks to Salesforce, software that had huge upfront costs before, suddenly became easy to purchase and easy to scale as necessary. Now, software as a service has become the standard in the software industry. Not just software but also computing power can be purchased as needed, for example from Amazon

[*] www.rolls-royce.com/media/press-releases-archive/yr-2012/121030-the-hour.aspx
[**] fsd.servicemax.com/2012/08/07/the-rolls-royce-of-field-service-is-rolls-royce/
[***] www.rolls-royce.com/media/our-stories/discover/2017/totalcare.aspx
[****] bebusinessed.com/history/the-history-of-saas/

Web Services and countless other companies. Whether a company sells software, food, heavy machinery or professional services, what used to be sold as products can be sold as subscriptions or services in any industry, if customers can benefit from it compared to the old model. And luckily subscriptions are not just great for customers, but financially compelling for companies if the shift from one-time fees to recurring revenue is done correctly. We will examine why it makes business sense to shift business models in the interviews with Zuora and Surf Air.

CONTINUOUS VALUE THROUGH SERVICE AGREEMENTS

A good example of a continuous service is the service offering of F-Secure, the European cyber security company. F-Secure used to sell cyber security products, but now they also package their products and professional services to provide companies with a continuous service, which includes rapid detection and response services for tracking and preventing security breaches. Instead of customers using only products to protect themselves, F-Secure now gives customers continuous value through services such as:

- Experienced threat hunters watching over a customer's environment all day, every day.

- Max 30 minutes from breach detection to response, as agreed in a Service Level Agreement.

- High-quality detections, with actionable response guidance by F-Secure experts[*]

In the next interview you'll gain insights about the subscription business model from John Phillips, the GM of EMEA for Zuora. Zuora is at the forefront of helping companies shift their business model from products to subscriptions. In the interview we'll discuss the financial benefit of moving to a subscription model and what some best-in-class companies are doing.

[*] https://www.f-secure.com/en/web/business_global/rapid-detection-and-response-service

INTERVIEW: JOHN PHILLIPS, GM OF EMEA AT ZUORA

Since its inception in 2007, Zuora has become the leading Subscription Economy® evangelist. Zuora is an enterprise software company that designs and sells SaaS applications for companies that have a subscription business model.

WHAT ARE THE MAIN DRIVERS OF THE SUBSCRIPTION ECONOMY?

There is a shift, and you have been able to feel it in the last 5–6 years in our personal lives and now we are starting to see that shift in B2B. Large businesses are changing how they consume and operate. Before the subscription economy, people had a fascination for owning things. If you go back about 120 years, the advent of mass production started this, for example the FORD MODEL T was launched in this era. Suddenly, we had factories building things and as a consumer you could own a TV, oven, or a car and really ever since then we have been fascinated by owning things.

Now people and companies are starting to realize that they don't want to purchase and own, but instead pay to gain access to the best technologies and better outcomes. Now there is a much higher rate of comfort in not owning because people have realized that whatever you buy (to own) is on a path to becoming obsolete from the moment you buy it, whether it be physical devices or software.

Consumers and businesses are smarter now about what they want and when they want it. They are fed up with products becoming obsolete, fed up of waiting and they want immediate fulfillment. They want things personalized and customized to their needs, they want experiences and things to be memorable. The service and outcome-driven world is this idea of the service being a living thing that you turn on one day and it gets better every day. We are not only seeing this in the consumer space but also in big business. Businesses want a similar concept applied to their world. I think the changes in leasing and financing in general are also impacting the subscription economy. The convergence of all these technologies available to us, for example Uber or Airbnb, has taught us that you can disrupt the ownership market.

WHAT ARE THE BUSINESS BENEFITS OF SHIFTING TO A SUBSCRIPTION BUSINESS MODEL?

The predictability of a recurring business model compared to an ad hoc traditional sales business is a difference of night and day, because of the way you can predict how you will perform financially looking forward. You can increase the 'stickiness' of the relationship with the customer and capture the whole lifetime value, create a larger potential market, create more up-sell and cross-sell opportunities, and provide personalized services that create lock-in like no other.

The subscription model is more predictable so it's easier to plan and make investments in marketing and sales. Additionally, business benefits can be derived when connecting products and devices, which can create new revenue streams. You can sell information to customers about how they are using the products to enhance their experience or you can sell anonymized aggregated data to 3rd parties that would love having access to new information that can help them improve their businesses.

WHAT IS THE BUSINESS OPPORTUNITY FOR TRADITIONAL COMPANIES?

This is a fantastic time and once-in-a-lifetime opportunity for some of these younger executives to make business transformations in these companies. If you look at the idea of a fleet of trucks for example, the relationship with the end customers is limited, and distribution happens through traditional channels. You build the product and push it out through your channels on multiple levels, then you get a customer. But with the advent of connected devices, a truck driver can be connected via 4G if the manufacturer makes applications for the driver. This is the first time for manufacturers to be able to build relationships with the end customers and enhance the end product as it is being used. The product might come from a traditional channel, but it can be enhanced directly. For lots of companies this is an opportunity to finally get to know who their customers are.

Getting to know the end customers produces an infinite amount of information that helps develop even more products and then we come to the question, what is the actual main product; is it the service or the product?

WHAT DO YOU SEE THAT THE BEST SUBSCRIPTION COMPANIES ARE DOING?

Look at companies like Google and Amazon. The business is not valued upon products, but based on subscriber IDs. Every subscription and ID is the valuation of the company. When you think of it this way, if the business is recurring and the customer willing to engage, then it doesn't matter what product you have, the relationship is open and you can put any product into that relationship.

As a company you should look at how you are organized and how you are structured. The bigger companies typically create a new division or create separate teams and separate innovation arms. You must separate the old and the new thinking. You need to look at changing the business processes and systems because otherwise the change will be too painful and hard.

The best companies are also not making it just about the product, it's about continuously giving the customer information that they can benefit from as part of the service. An example from the B2C world that can be applied to B2B is an example of a dog food company, which is a customer of ours. They provide information to dog owners about what kinds of toys and accessories suit the type of dog that they have. By doing this they are creating more value for their customers than their competitors are creating.

ARE ALL COMPANIES CHANGING FROM PRODUCT TO SUBSCRIPTION MODEL?

In five or ten years from now, will companies stop selling products and literally deliver everything as a service, yes quite possibly in most cases. In some cases, for either legal or practical reasons this won't happen.

Making the shift takes many steps. For many there are big financial issues with credit and leasing and commercial concepts, but don't underestimate the power of the subscription economy to enhance services around physical products. Because when the products were not connected, they were isolated, and there are very few products designed today that are not connected, whether it's flooring or light bulbs. Everything you look at could be connected.

New services will be created around products with the goal of enhancing the experience of using the products. I believe manufacturers will want to own this element, because if you give that up then you may have lost this once-in-an-era opportunity to make a huge positive change in your business.

WHAT ARE THE CHALLENGES OR MISTAKES THAT YOU SEE COMPANIES MAKING?

The mistake often being made is the thinking that to have a subscription model you must have a digital service. Well, actually, you should be thinking that almost every physical product could be enhanced by software. The user experience could be improved by additional information.

We are all still tied into an old business model. It's a model that is harder to unpick than we would think. If you think of the structure, you have some concept of a production unit, manufacturing and research and development (R&D). The concept is to create a hit product and almost all company structures are built around building the product and detecting which sales channels the product could be sold in and then you push it out. When you get enough channels, you get a good margin and then start driving the cost down. This is the traditional model and it is quite tough to change it.

WHAT IS YOUR ADVICE FOR COMPANIES THAT WANT TO MOVE TO A SUBSCRIPTION BUSINESS MODEL?

Build trust. A lot of the best companies are working on how they can build more trust with customers. How will you get customers to have recurring payments from their accounts? You need to think about why your customers would be willing to enter a recurring relationship. It doesn't matter if it's a small or large amount, creating a regular payment is a massive hurdle. Customers are not necessarily comfortable with their credit card information in the hands of companies, or having a close a relationship with a company.

Another piece of advice is not to just change the product from the way the payment is being made from a perpetual one-time cost to X dollars a month, because then you are missing the point. The point is that customers can have a more personal and flexible service so that every customer can customize the package they use.

HOW WILL SALES AND MARKETING NEED TO CHANGE WHEN MOVING OVER TO SELLING SUBSCRIPTIONS?

Firstly, they will need to think differently about how you measure the business. Don't think about new sales, think about annual recurring revenue growth. Don't think about units sold, think about usage. Bundle and price your products around usage and value. Don't think about cost plus pricing which is the classical model, instead think about value-based pricing. Don't think about channel optimization, think about customer experience optimization. Focus on how you can build a sticky relationship with customers; don't worry so much about the channels.

Be prepared to iterate often and find your way to success in an agile matter. Don't spend six months analyzing customers and coming up with a perfect pricing model. Just throw it out there and test your way to the right pricing model, because you will get data on what customers are willing to pay much faster by taking this approach.

Focus more on holding onto customers, don't focus only on new customer acquisition. Build relationships, not customers. A customer database is not enough, the relationship is a different concept.

See more about this in Chapter 10 –
Marketing and customer success become crucial

WHAT ARE THE KEY METRICS THAT SHOULD GUIDE THE BUSINESS?

Some key financial metrics are monthly recurring revenue (MRR), annual contract value (ACV) and annual recurring revenue (ARR).

A couple of good metrics to use for guiding sales and marketing activities are customer acquisition costs (CAC) and net retention rate (NRR) which tells us about churn.

A good churn rate is below 10%. Net retention rate is a useful one for shareholders and analysts, because it tells us what we have if we do not acquire new customers. So, it helps to answer the question: what would happen if we didn't have a sales and marketing team getting new customers? Since good recurring revenue models always have up-sell and cross-sell opportunities for current customers, you should be able to grow the business even without acquiring new customers, if the churn is kept at a low enough level.

Once you get the equation right, the spending on sales and marketing is in essence more about how fast you want to grow because you're able to predict where you will end up. If you want to go up from 1M to 5M, you can go fast and grab the market, if your net retention rate is at a good enough level.

FROM A TECHNOLOGY PERSPECTIVE, WHAT NEEDS TO BE CONSIDERED WHEN SHIFTING TO A SUBSCRIPTION MODEL?

If you look at how systems were built for the old business model, for example how things were done in the 80s, you had relational databases, then ERP, and not long after that CRM. These systems were designed for the product mentality. ERP is about handling an order that's finite. You take an order, you invoice it, bill it, deliver it and close it. Done! In the subscription world this does not occur because the lifecycle of an order is fundamentally different because the order never goes away or at least it has many stages of life before ending. For example, there may also be multiple tiers of service that are packaged for customers. During the lifecycle the number of users and level of package could change. The lifecycle is long and complex. For this reason, companies need technology that sits between ERP and traditional CRM because it will help with this.

A subscription is unlike a product sale, because it lives, exists and is constantly changing. Every time you change it, the systems need to be able to manage this. In the front end, on e-commerce platforms, it was quite difficult to make the necessary changes. For example, launching a campaign with special pricing for a certain type of customer segment would be a horrendous change for traditional systems to manage because they have a very sequential order to cash process, where every part of the process is tied together rigidly.

OUTCOMES AS A SERVICE

What you heard in the interview with John Phillips from Zuora is that essentially anything can be sold with a subscription model, not just easily digitized things such as software, movies, books and music, but also physical products. What is now changing is the drive towards lower CAPEX and more OPEX type of financing in businesses, which is creating demand for subscription services in all industries, not just the traditional subscription industries like media or insurance.

CAPEX – Capital expenditure are funds used by a company to acquire, upgrade, and maintain physical assets such as property, industrial buildings, or equipment. CAPEX is often used to undertake new projects or investments by the firm.[*]

OPEX – Operating expenses are the costs for a company to run its business operations day to day.[**]

Purchasers in companies are more willing to subscribe to the end-product i.e. value-based models if there is a competitive provider for that in a market. In businesses, especially in software, we have seen this transformation in purchasing happening during the past twenty years as software companies have started offering a subscription model for something that was capital intensive earlier.

Twenty years ago, the subscription model was good for companies that did not have that much capital, such as startups. Larger companies with lots of capital had a difficult time justifying the investment in SaaS solutions as the cost would be paid again and again every year compared to traditional software which – in theory – was purchased once and then amortized every year until the software did not cost anything any longer.

Here is what General Electric (GE) thinks about the outcome-based model:

"This service model can be attractive to both the buyer and provider. It simplifies the buyer's world, and if customers don't receive the guaranteed outcomes, then they don't pay (and can even charge penalties in some cases). Sellers, meanwhile, take on risk but create value by solving complexities and pricing the service based on value created. This ease of doing business can improve relationships with customers, while integrating profitable long-term service and maintenance activities into the contract."[***]

This new model of providing customers with more outcomes is connected more to customer value, which means that the customer pays the vendor as they attain value. For example, instead of selling a machine, the value of the service can

[*]   Learn more about CAPEX here: www.investopedia.com/terms/c/capitalexpenditure.asp
[**] Learn more about OPEX here: www.investopedia.com/ask/answers/020915/what-difference-between-capex-and-opex.asp
[***] www.ge.com/power/transform/article.transform.articles.2017.oct.the-outcome-as-a-service-model

be measured as tons per month of something or megawatts per hour/day/week/month, or the customer can use the asset as much as they want with a fixed price. In this new model, the customer is subscribing to a stream of value. Potential capital intensiveness is managed by another party and the vendor is locked into providing value with the most innovative and optimal ways it can. An example of this would also be European-based energy company Solnet, a leading provider of smart solar solutions for B2B customers. Solnet has decided to build their offering to create value for customers as quickly as possible, while minimizing the customers' risks. They have an outcome-based model so customers know what they will pay, instead of making costly upfront investments. Country Manager Veli-Matti Heimonen stated in an interview with us:

"Customers don't always want to own products or buy projects, they want value right away, and they want the value at a minimal risk. Everyone is so busy now that achieving the value cannot be complex, we must make it easy to buy and easy to benefit from our service."

The outcome-based approach can be used for creating more value and partnering with customers in product segments that were not possible before. One example of a company that has made a shift towards the outcome-based business model is an 80-year-old company called Kennametal, a manufacturer of machine tooling and mining equipment. They used to have a very transactional relationship with their customers until they built a 'shared rewards' business model. Kennametal now gathers and analyzes data to discover how their tools and machines are being used, so that they can give recommendations for customers to improve their operations. Instead of selling products, Kennametal helps customers increase productivity, and shares the savings with their customers that are factories, mining operators or vehicle fleet owners.[*]

GETTING CLOSER TO CUSTOMERS CREATES GROWTH AND MORE PROFITS

Margins are being squeezed in every part of the value chain, but those that are controlling the customer relationship and are closer to providing outcomes for customers are set to make the most profits. All other parts of the value chain are slowly being dried up from profits through commoditization. Moving up in the value chain doesn't automatically transfer to higher margins. Even if some companies have the capability to offer full outcomes, if customers do not trust them enough, then they will not have success, because the outcome-based model requires an entirely new level of cooperation and access to critical information that needs to be exchanged when monitoring the use of machinery or software.

[*] Learn more about Kennametal here: www.industryweek.com/growth-strategies/new-go-market-model-industrial-internet

In the next graph we've depicted the spectrum from selling products to providing outcomes to customers. Instead of buying a new piece of machinery, the customer can pay for the machine through a lease agreement, subscription or an outcome if they only want to move a set amount of dirt from place A to B. This same graph can be applied to buying a piece of machinery that creates purified drinking water from dirty water. On the left side of the spectrum the customer buys the machine. As we move to the right the customer buys the machine with a maintenance contract, and gets some help now and then from a person who can help with the chemical applications. Far to the right they would have someone operate the machine and pay per liter of water that is purified, with a set price.

The closer a company is to offering outcomes to customers, the more customers are willing to pay, since the value of the service increases. Combine this with a continuous and predictable relationship with the customer and the business will not just be more profitable, it will also be more predictable. Customers are happier and the business is more profitable.

A good example of this is Rolls-Royce with its TotalCare® offering. Today over half of Rolls-Royce's revenues and around 70% of its profits come from their TotalCare® service business model.[*]

VALUE CHAIN: FROM PRODUCT TO OUTCOME

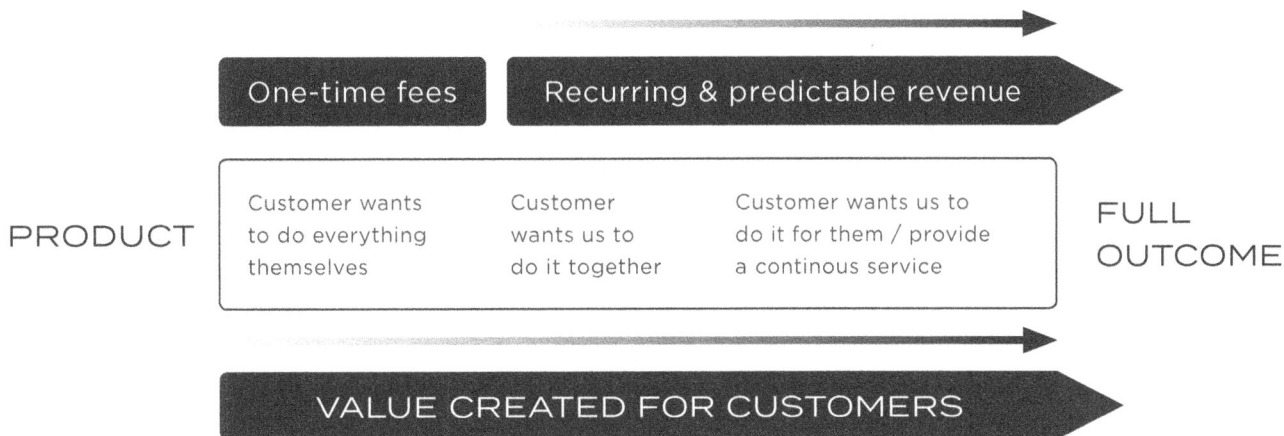

One-time fees	Recurring & predictable revenue →

| PRODUCT | Customer wants to do everything themselves | Customer wants us to do it together | Customer wants us to do it for them / provide a continous service | FULL OUTCOME |

VALUE CREATED FOR CUSTOMERS →

* Tim Jones, Dave McCormick, Caroline Dewing, Growth Champions, p.186

CHAPTER 3

/ GROWTH FROM SOFTWARE AND SERVICES

In chapter 2 we established that customers want more flexibility, more options, and less risk and that several different business models exist for achieving this. These changes in customer behavior and needs are exactly what is creating growth for many B2B companies that offer services and software. Revenue from services and software is very different than revenue from products because services and software are often recurring and more profitable as well.

A good example comes from Tien Tzuo, the CEO of Zuora, in his book, Subscribed. He explains the example of Cisco, the communications giant, who decided to fully commit to growing the business through recurring services. Instead of changing their basic products to subscriptions they started building services around their product offering. Their hardware now comes embedded with machine learning and analytics software, which helps their customers. Today, almost a third of Cisco revenue is recurring.[*] In the book, Subscribed, he also points out that GE used to sell light bulbs, electronic fixtures etc. and now most of GE's revenues come from services, not products. GE was #4 on the Fortune 500 list in 1955 and it's now still at #13 (fall of 2017). Another example was IBM that has become a business services company, not a product manufacturer.

GROWTH FROM SOFTWARE AND SERVICES

In order to offer outcomes or solutions as close to outcomes as possible, software and services are needed and this is a huge growth opportunity for traditional companies selling products. Tzuo points out: "What these companies are realizing is that IoT enables them to view their products as whole systems, as opposed to individual units that are sold to strangers."[**]

These all-in-one systems are allowing companies to create more value for customers. The companies that provide these more complete systems clearly have an advantage over competitors selling only products, or products and services that are not connected to each other. The competitive advantage and growth enabler for companies is their relationship with customers, the information they have about customers, and how that information is being used. Companies that really know their customers well are pure service companies, like professional service organizations (lawyers, architects, financial advisors, consultants). These companies have a great growth opportunity in creating scalable software products instead of only selling billable hours and consulting projects.

[*] Tien Tzuo, Subscribed, p. 12.
[**] Tien Tzuo, Subscribed, p. 106.

These firms are already so close to their customers that they know their problems and challenges better than anyone else. This means that they are in a good position to innovate and create software to sell to their customers. For example, an architect agency could create software to simplify the early stages of the planning process for designing a building.

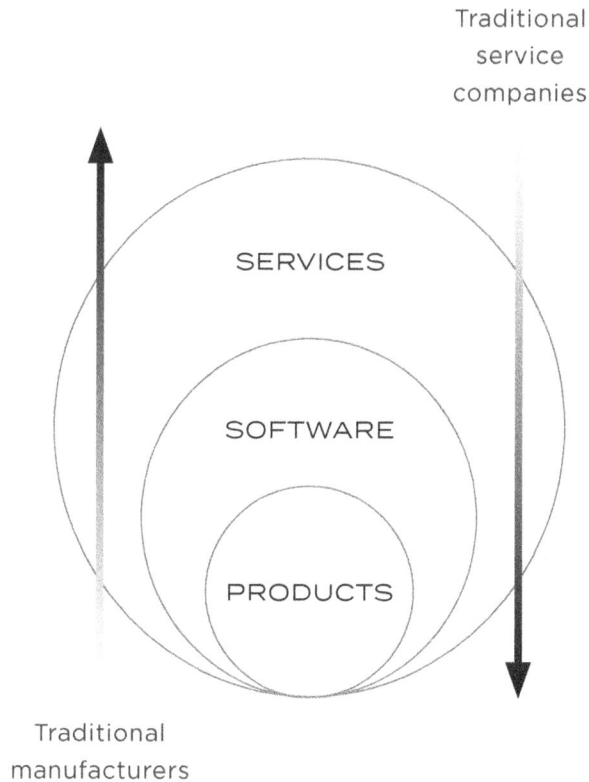

Traditional
service
companies

SERVICES

SOFTWARE

PRODUCTS

Traditional
manufacturers

CONNECTED SYSTEMS ENABLE NEW PRODUCT AND SERVICE INNOVATIONS

Combining the power of software, data and hardware is something that all companies can do. Why can't a manufacturer have a similar ecosystem of applications as Apple, for example? Software companies are creating huge economic impacts, as other companies can now build applications on top of their platforms and connect applications via open APIs (Application programming interface) No matter what industry or what type of product, in the future every product will have an open API that software can be built around. Everything will be connected.

This is what Gartner says about API's

"APIs make it easier to integrate and connect people, places, systems, data, things and algorithms, create new user experiences, share data and information, authenticate people and things, enable transactions and algorithms, leverage third-party algorithms, and create new product/ services and business models." *

CASE: CATERPILLAR – THINKING BEYOND TRADITIONAL PRODUCTS

For 90 years Caterpillar was coming up with innovations that were focused on their machinery. Now Caterpillar's innovation revolves around the data that machinery produces. Realizing that capturing information about how the equipment was being operated could transform how much value customers got from using Caterpillar's equipment, they started developing connectivity to their equipment. Their CEO Douglas Oberhelman said at an annual shareholders meeting that they should start thinking "beyond the yellow iron" and in 2014 Caterpillar launched its Cat Connect capability. Instead of selling machinery, the value proposition became about improving productivity, profits, safety and environmental efficiency.

To make this shift there were many changes that had to be made. For one, Caterpillar had to launch a new division called Analytics & Innovation, that oversaw the development of new digital business models. This new division became crucial because it allowed Caterpillar to develop new innovations faster. As Caterpillar's former Chief Data Officer said in an article, "while it takes three to five years to design and build a new bulldozer, in the world of data analytics, new product development is measured in days and weeks." In the same article he emphasized the importance of speed, noting that otherwise "we will be disrupted by companies moving faster than us."

Caterpillar also formed a joined venture with a predictive analytics company, to be able to develop a solution that would enable customers to know ahead of time when equipment was breaking down, and thus avoiding the costly down-time of machinery not working at the construction or mining site.[*]

PRODUCT TO OUTCOME LEVELS

In the next graph there are four levels that help identify how close a company is to offering outcomes to their customers. The companies that can move from level 1 up to level 3–4 will become more profitable, while the ones that cannot make the shift will fight to remain profitable in the future. The example in the graph is of a manufacturing company, but these four levels with a bit of creativity can be applied to almost any business.

The more of a partner a company is to its customers, the more they know about their customers and the more likely they are to be able to offer some types of services with outcomes that both parties can commit to.

[*] www.industryweek.com/growth-strategies/new-go-market-model-industrial-internet

PRODUCT TO OUTCOME LEVELS

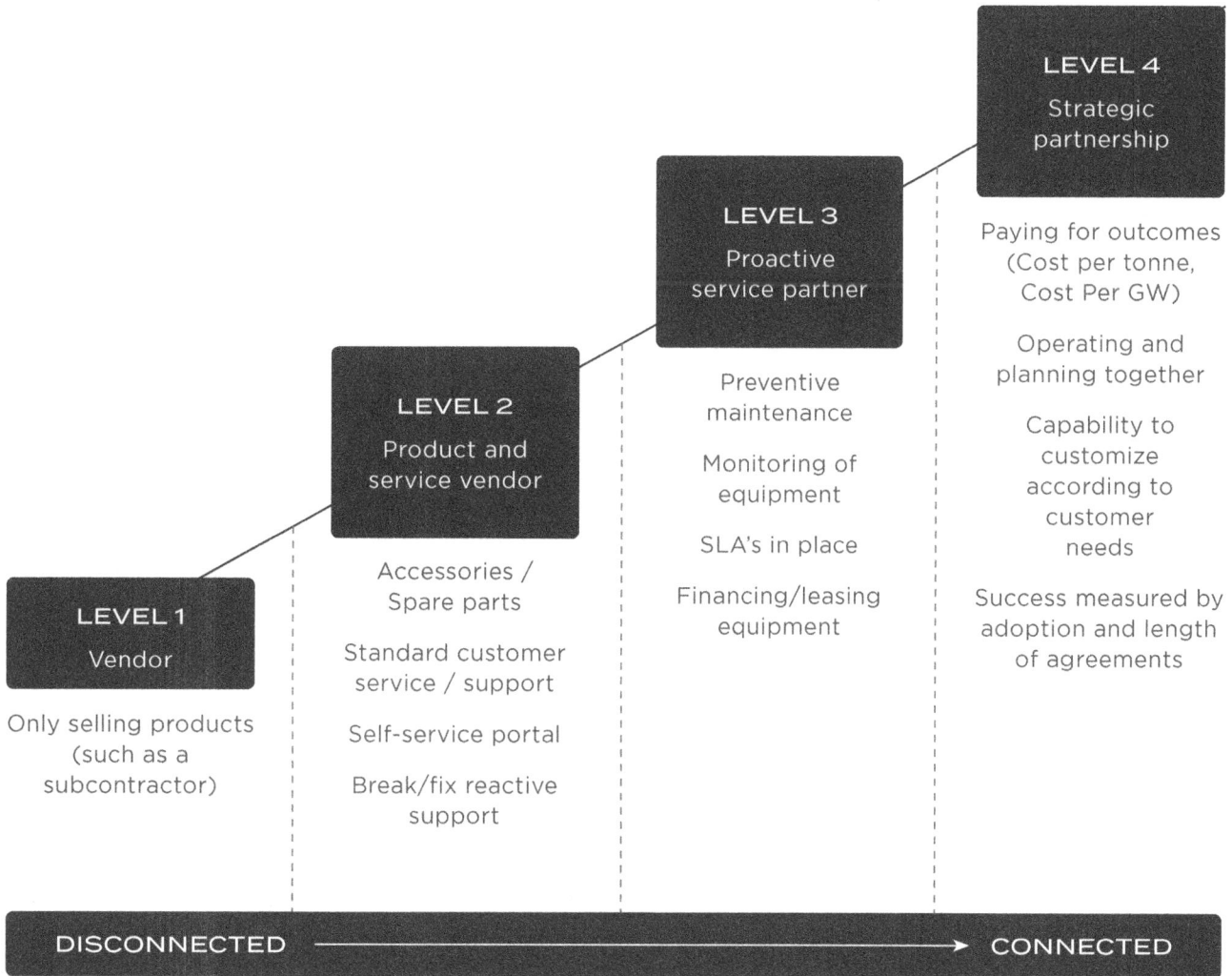

LEVEL 4
Strategic partnership

Paying for outcomes (Cost per tonne, Cost Per GW)

Operating and planning together

Capability to customize according to customer needs

Success measured by adoption and length of agreements

LEVEL 3
Proactive service partner

Preventive maintenance

Monitoring of equipment

SLA's in place

Financing/leasing equipment

LEVEL 2
Product and service vendor

Accessories / Spare parts

Standard customer service / support

Self-service portal

Break/fix reactive support

LEVEL 1
Vendor

Only selling products (such as a subcontractor)

DISCONNECTED → CONNECTED

THE SHIFT TO SUBSCRIPTIONS OR OUTCOMES IS VERY CHALLENGING

Even though companies want to sell outcomes to customers, there are often many challenges due to the current organizational structure and financial reporting.

The conflict comes from the difference of profit and loss units that sometimes compete against each other. A manufacturer or a provider of some type of product or service should be thinking about how to cannibalize its own profitable spare part business, as an example. For many companies, it could be a good idea to establish an independent and separate company or unit to cannibalize its old product-centric business, because the risk is that otherwise a competitor will go ahead and do it.

There is also a conflict for some companies in simple things like creating preventive maintenance contracts if they have a large market share and a large install base. Ad hoc service visits for this type of company can be more profitable at first glance – especially looking short-term - because the customer wants a problem to be fixed right away (so their willingness to pay is higher), as opposed to preventive maintenance programs. Spare parts are highly profitable, and even more profitable when the customer needs them right way in order to continue with their operations.

It takes more sales focus to get preventive maintenance contracts sold, as opposed to ad hoc spare parts and single service visits. Selling services is therefore radically different from selling products and responding to customers ad hoc needs, because it requires a more strategic approach to selling. If we use the levels in the previous graph, a company on level 1 or level 2 does not have the capabilities or processes in place to sell preventive maintenance contracts or outcome-based partnership models, like level-3 and level-4 companies do.

An example of a company that had to go through a big transformation to move from products to outcomes is Xerox. Their standard products were becoming commoditized and they had to find a way to create more value for their clients. They knew they needed to move from selling products to outcomes to ensure they remained competitive. Xerox created a service called 'Managed Print Services'. The service meant that Xerox started managing fleets of printers and other devices; not just Xerox products, but also the products produced and sold by other companies. Xerox started managing the maintenance, upgrades, paper and toner replenishment. Under Managed Print Services, clients only pay for pages printed, which means a simpler experience and lower operating cost. At the time, it was a radical business model change for Xerox, because it required changing how they worked in almost all their functions, like sales, marketing, supply chain, field service, and product engineering. They also had to develop a key capability which was how they collected data and used analytics for monitoring the fleet. In the end, this transformation from product to outcome created tremendous value by aligning incentives between Xerox and its customers.[*]

Next, we will dive into the interview with Surf Air Europe's CEO Simon Talling-Smith to hear how the company is changing an industry that has been operating in a very similar way for decades. You will get insight into what it takes to change business models and why some companies are struggling to shift their business model.

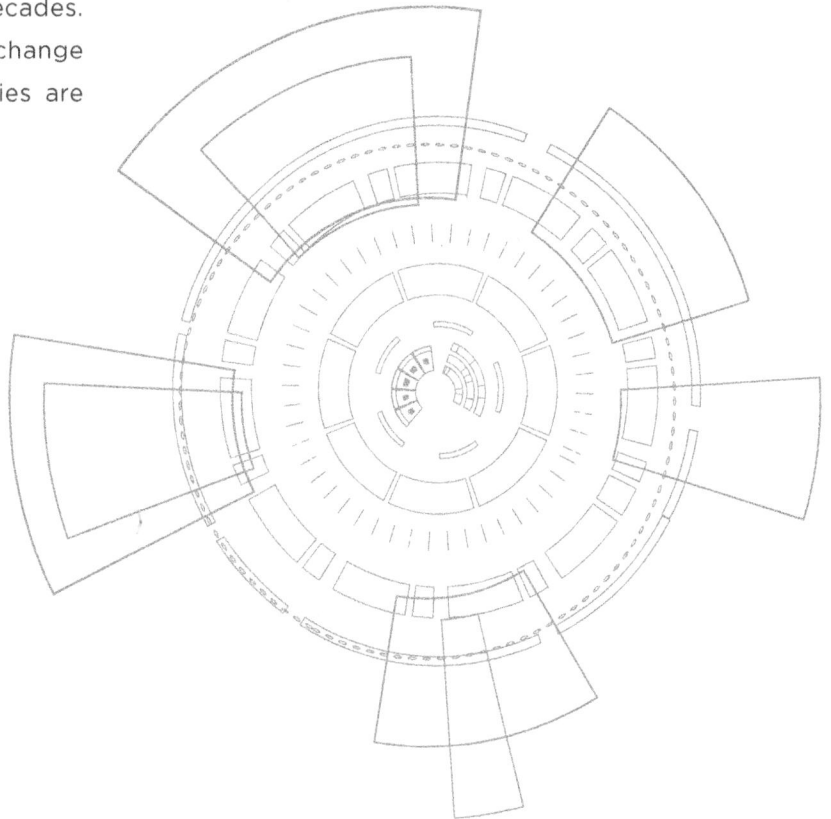

[*] blogs.parc.com/2015/06/stop-selling-products-and-offer-outcome-based-services-instead

INTERVIEW:
SIMON TALLING-SMITH, CEO OF SURF AIR EUROPE

ABOUT SURF AIR
Surf Air is a commuter airline that offers unlimited flight service for a fixed monthly fee, both in the United States and Europe.

WHAT ARE THE MAIN BENEFITS TO YOUR CUSTOMERS WHEN SUBSCRIBING TO YOUR SERVICES INSTEAD OF BUYING THEM THE OLD-FASHIONED WAY?

There is certainly an economic benefit for frequent fliers because the unit price falls, so frequent fliers like that. Secondly, it's super easy. Using our simple app is much easier than the traditional way. Think about the number of screens you must go through to book a regular ticket even if that starts from a place like Kayak, because you are directed to the airline site where you must go through the outbound page, look at different fair categories, as well as departure and arrival options. After this you want to look and compare different options. You end up going through screen after screen just to make one purchase. It's complicated also later because then half-way through your trip you realize you need to change the ticket, then you've got to go back to the site. Then there's change penalties, and you must ring the call center, and it's all a timely and costly hassle. With the subscription model we are not pricing any of our seats. All our seats are basically free and we do not overbook so our booking system is very simple. We can produce a super-friendly app for our members, and in three taps the flight is booked within 30 seconds.

Another big benefit is predictability of costs because most of our customers are flying for business reasons. They don't need to think whether they can afford another extra flight and they also avoid all the other hassles. Everything is taken care of.

WHAT ARE THE BUSINESS BENEFITS OF OFFERING YOUR SERVICES AS A SUBSCRIPTION?

It's dead simple, it's both continuity and predictability of revenue, so we know what our revenue will be every month.

"As we build up the members, we haven't just sold individual one-time seats that month, we have made a customer for a long time, as long as we keep them happy."

I think there is also an often-overlooked benefit of subscriptions, in that there is an indirect benefit for customers and the company. The difference between a traditional commercial airline model and the Surf Air model is radical. What traditional airlines are doing is optimizing the revenue of every aircraft that flies and they have incredibly complex algorithms and armies of people just optimizing the pricing. In the subscription model we are not doing that at all. What we are trying to manage is the average price that subscribers pay us and then looking after the longevity of the relationship. Because of the commercial model we are highly motivated to keep our customers happy. Members leaving us is the equivalent of an empty plane for a traditional airline.

I think there is an indirect benefit, both for companies and their customers, in the subscription model because there is now more focus on ensuring the relationship is working, as opposed to the more transactional business model.

WHAT DO YOU THINK ARE THE MAIN REASONS THAT SOME COMPANIES ARE STRUGGLING WITH CHANGING THEIR BUSINESS MODEL TO BECOMING SUBSCRIPTION-BASED?

The main thing is that the two business models are different and it's quite hard, or almost impossible to do a bit of both. You cannot subscribe one half and then revenue manage the other half. What I found hard from moving from commercial to Surf Air, was that I had to completely unlearn many things I had learned in the past 20 years. The hardest thing to unlearn was the revenue optimization per aircraft, thinking through individual seats, and their distribution. It's very hard for people in that old world to start thinking about the new world. It's like speaking Japanese and German at the same time. This is probably the biggest barrier and reason why traditional airlines will not embrace the subscription model.

FROM A SALES AND MARKETING STANDPOINT, WHAT NEEDS TO CHANGE WHEN MOVING OVER TO A SUBSCRIPTION MODEL FROM A TRADITIONAL PRODUCT AND SERVICE MODEL?

The biggest difference is that you need a much longer view of the customer. Traditional companies treat their customers as one-time events. If they are lucky they can tie those one-time events together via a frequent flyer card. But in the subscription business you have true members. Once you have a membership philosophy then you understand that members expect a lot more than one-time customers. You must be able to deliver on those expectations. You need to have the right attitude running through the entire organization and one of the core beliefs needs to be delivering on member expectations. Secondly, you must make sure you have the right systems and processes in place to be able to deliver this.

See more about this in Chapter 9 –
Re-designing roles to support the customer journey and Chapter 10 – Marketing and customer success become crucial.

HOW HAVE YOU ORGANIZED YOUR FRONTLINE EMPLOYEES TO BE ABLE TO RUN THIS TYPE OF ORGANIZATION? (SALES, MARKETING, AND CUSTOMER SERVICE)

We have a team of frontline employees, from the initiation of first contact which belongs to our sales team; they are responsible for spreading the word and getting people to make the decision to join. Once prospects become members, our membership team takes over. They look after our members by phone and even meet them face-to-face in the airports in which we operate. We, of course, also stay in touch with our members via our blog, newsletter and the usual social channels like Facebook and Instagram. We are also working on putting different types of metrics in place for the membership team to proactively manage customers who could perhaps be at risk of leaving.

See more about this in Chapter 9 –
Re-designing roles to support the customer journey

DO YOU MANAGE ALL YOUR CUSTOMER RELATIONSHIPS THE SAME WAY OR DO YOU HAVE DIFFERENT TYPES OF CUSTOMER MANAGEMENT MODELS?

In the acquisition stage we try to be as targeted as possible, but broadly maintaining a similar approach. We manage all our members in the same way. All our customers are worth the same amount of money, because the monthly membership fee is the same.

See more about this in Chapter 6 –
Customer segmentation

WHAT ARE THE KEY METRICS YOU ARE USING TO DEVELOP THE BUSINESS?

Churn, new acquisition and average price. These are the three key metrics we look at. Pretty simple!

WHAT IS YOUR ADVICE FOR COMPANIES THAT DO NOT HAVE A SUBSCRIPTION BUSINESS MODEL YET?

You need to make sure that there is a repeat market for your product or that you can at least base a slice of your business on that market. Secondly, create a new product line, a new business line, a new sub-brand of the business and allow it to build up a subscription model. It's better to cannibalize the business yourself than let someone else do it.

SURF AIR IS OFTEN REFERRED TO AS THE "UBER OF THE SKIES", SO THAT MUST MEAN YOU HAVE A LOT OF CUSTOMER INTERACTION TO MANAGE. WHAT IS THE ROLE OF CRM AND MARKETING AUTOMATION IN YOUR BUSINESS?

We use the expected acquisition tools like Salesforce. Our CRM, in terms of automation, is fairly limited, but as I see Surf Air growing in the next 1-5 years and as we move from managing a fairly easy audience of members, to many more, then the role of technology will grow. When we have tens of thousands of members, our CRM capability will be super important. At this point we are making sure that we already know what capabilities and data we will need when the business is bigger, so that we can execute our business while keeping our future needs in mind.

See more about this in Chapter 11 –
Technology components of your Growth Platform

Moving from selling products to recurring revenue makes the business not only more predictable, it also makes it more valuable. But, it is evident that many CFOs and investors will not likely be happy as the revenue that was once recognized immediately, is now coming later. Adobe, Cisco and other companies that are thinking long term and building recurring services have taken a hit short term, but long term they are more stable. This is the shift that software companies have had to make, as they move to subscriptions from one-time purchases. A new set of financial metrics is needed to analyze and develop companies that sell recurring services and products, but additionally a longer-term view is needed, and this puts focus on the entire lifecycle of the product or service in use for the customer.

What has changed is that work doesn't stop when the contract is signed, but rather continues during the whole time that the customer is using the service or product. This is interesting because the focus on a customer lifecycle is also what is needed, as customers are demanding a better experience from the companies they are working with. In the next chapter we will tackle the topic of customer experience.

CHAPTER 4

/ THE MODERN CUSTOMER EXPECTS MORE

We now live in an information-rich society, where 500 hours of YouTube videos are uploaded and 1,440 WordPress posts are shared per minute. That's 720,000 hours of video per day and 2,073,600 WordPress posts per day.[*] Customers have access to a wealth of information about products and prices from vendors all over the world that they did not have before. Boundaries to do business have nearly vanished, and it's creating pressure on companies that once used to have great margins. In some industries customers cannot distinguish products from each other, by other factors than price, which is called commoditization. Since products and services are becoming commoditized, companies must compete on other factors.

Instead of innovating new products or services or improving the experience for customers, some companies have been pouring more money into advertising, to stay top of mind with customers. There is so much marketing everywhere that customers are becoming blind to random and generic marketing. In 1994, AT&T made internet history by running the very first banner ad that recorded a click-through rate of 43%. Today, the average click-through rate (CTR) for a banner ad weighs in at less than 1%.[**] It's not just marketing, but also sales that is being ignored. One study shows that only 1% of cold calls result in an appointment.[***] Getting through to a customer via the phone is getting harder and email as well, with only 24% of sales emails opened.[****]

Customers do not need to rely on sales for basic information any longer. They have high expectations for speed of service, and web experience, and when they do talk to sales people, the expectation for added value is high. With regards to speed of services, one study stated that 9% of customers expect an answer on social media within 5 minutes, 11% within 15 minutes and 12% within 30 minutes.[*****]

WE NOW LIVE IN THE 'AGE OF THE CUSTOMER'

A while back when you wanted to see advanced technology you would have be at your office or at an innovation lab, not at home. It's interesting to see how fast this has turned around, because now you have the newest gadgets and technology at home, not at work. An internet connection and a decent device gives you access to the world's wonders. Customers hold more information than

[*] martech.zone/how-much-content-online-60-sec
[**] www.forbes.com/sites/forbesagencycouncil/2016/08/23/is-content-blindness-the-new-banner-blindness/#7d129f8e4f84
[***] www.baylor.edu/content/services/document.php/183060.pdf#page=2
[****] blog.topohq.com/sales-development-technology-the-stack-emerges/
[*****] www.groovehq.com/support/customer-support-statistics

ever, and this information has made customers extremely empowered in the past years. A few years ago Forrester Research published their 'Age of the Customer' report. In the report they explain how we have arrived in this time, which they named the Age of the Customer and what phases we have gone through before this age. The three earlier phases where the age of manufacturing, distribution and information. It is a great way of explaining the transformations we've gone through from a societal and business perspective. To see a graph of this timeline go to Google or Slideshare and you'll find many different variations of The Age of the Customer. Many companies are still set up for the age of distribution or age of information, and are playing catch up to the Age of the Customer. The old days were all about product innovations, followed by innovations of logistics or some type of new way of distributing products to customers. Now we are in the time when our innovations need to be centered around the customers. Either these are product innovations around how customers can consume and use our products and services differently to benefit themselves more, or innovations around marketing, sales and service to create a better buying experience.

HOW MODERN CUSTOMERS BUY

It's mainly price and product transparency that is impacting B2B buying the most. Sales as a profession is not going to disappear, but it is changing form. In later chapters we'll discuss more about how the sales profession has changed and where it is developing. Here are some statistics on buyer behavior that demonstrate how B2B buying has changed.

47% of buyers viewed 3-5 pieces of content before engaging with a sales rep.[*]

B2B buyers are 57% of the way through their buying research before first contacting the seller.[**]

93% of B2B buying processes start with an online search.[***]

As customers have become more independent, companies have adjusted their approach by using digital marketing to take care of the beginning of the funnel.

79% of top-performing companies have been using marketing automation for three or more years.[*****]

[*] www.demandgenreport.com/resources/research/2016-content-preferences-survey-b2b-buyers-value-content-that-offers-data-and-analysis
[**] www.cebglobal.com/marketing-communications/digital-evolution.html
[***] interfacedigital.co.za/50-key-digital-statistics-worth-shouting-about-part-1/
[****] ozcontent.com/blog/marketing-automation-strategies-increase-email-lead-generation/
[*****] blog.marketo.com/2015/08/data-talks-2-proven-lead-generation-tactics-to-jump-on-now.html
[******] www.business2community.com/infographics/marketing-automation-by-the-numbers-infographic-0342287#!rFqTU

93% of B2B companies say content marketing generates more leads than traditional marketing strategies.[******]

Businesses that use marketing automation to nurture prospects experience a 451% increase in qualified leads.[*******]

Due to the changes in customer behavior, B2B companies are shifting focus from being purely field sales focused to marketing and customer experience focused.

> "Customers are 5.2X more likely to purchase from companies with a great customer experience"

hmedia.dmnews.com/images/2013/09/23/cx_infographic_full_size_463272.png (Temkin Group)

CUSTOMER EXPERIENCE HAS BECOME A PRIORITY

5.2X seems like a crazy statistic and it is certainly hard to agree or disagree when most people don't agree on what customer experience means in practice. For now, we can define that customer experience is every interaction that the customer has with a company in one way or another, in one channel or another. We will dive deeper into customer experience in many later sections of this book and at this point we will examine why customer experience has become such a key priority for most leading companies.

A Forrester study found that:

> "72% of businesses say that improving customer experience is their top priority."

www.forrester.com/72+Of+Businesses+Name+Improving+Customer+Experience+Their+Top+Priority/-/E-PRE9109

Many mistakenly think of customer experience as customer service. Customer experience is a topic that surfaces in the next interview with Mikko Leinonen from KONE at the end of this chapter. Mikko defines customer experience as: "the sum of all the interactions with the customer along their journey."

EMOTIONS AND CUSTOMER EXPERIENCE

As human beings we are still mainly driven by our need to survive, and therefore we are guided by our emotions. Having a nice car or a beautiful home is for most not necessarily about shelter and transportation, but about a luxury lifestyle that means a better and healthier life. A higher status means a higher probability of surviving.

That we are guided by our emotions is what keeps us alive. From this perspective it makes perfect sense that the experience that customers have when buying a product or using a service is key, because buying is always an emotional experience. This emotional connection is the factor that is most often overlooked, especially in B2B. When you realize that customers have more control of their options and consider how humans are wired, it makes sense that customer experience is becoming a priority for companies.

Something that also ties into emotions and customer experience, is that humans want to belong to something. Customer experience is not only limited to the different touchpoints, but also that by being a customer an individual feels that they are a part of something, that they belong to a community. Even if someone doesn't go to the gym as often as they should, they are paying for the feeling that they are part of something. The same goes for a country club. The idea is that you belong to something by being a member, or that buying a product puts you in a type of lifestyle category. Even though the product or service is not being used, it's a feeling that you are constantly part of something that you are also paying for.

B2B companies should bring their customers onto customer advisory boards and make sure they are a partner that customers want to be associated with, not just for the products and services. In the next graph this is the level-4 customer-obsessed companies that are doing this.

One way of determining the customer-centricity of a company is to evaluate how connected a company is with its customers. In even more detail we would want to evaluate how connected a company is to its customers via its people, systems and products.

To make it easier to reflect and evaluate how connected and customer-centric a company is we have created a four-stage model with some ideas about typical attributes of companies in each stage.

CUSTOMER CENTRICITY LEVELS

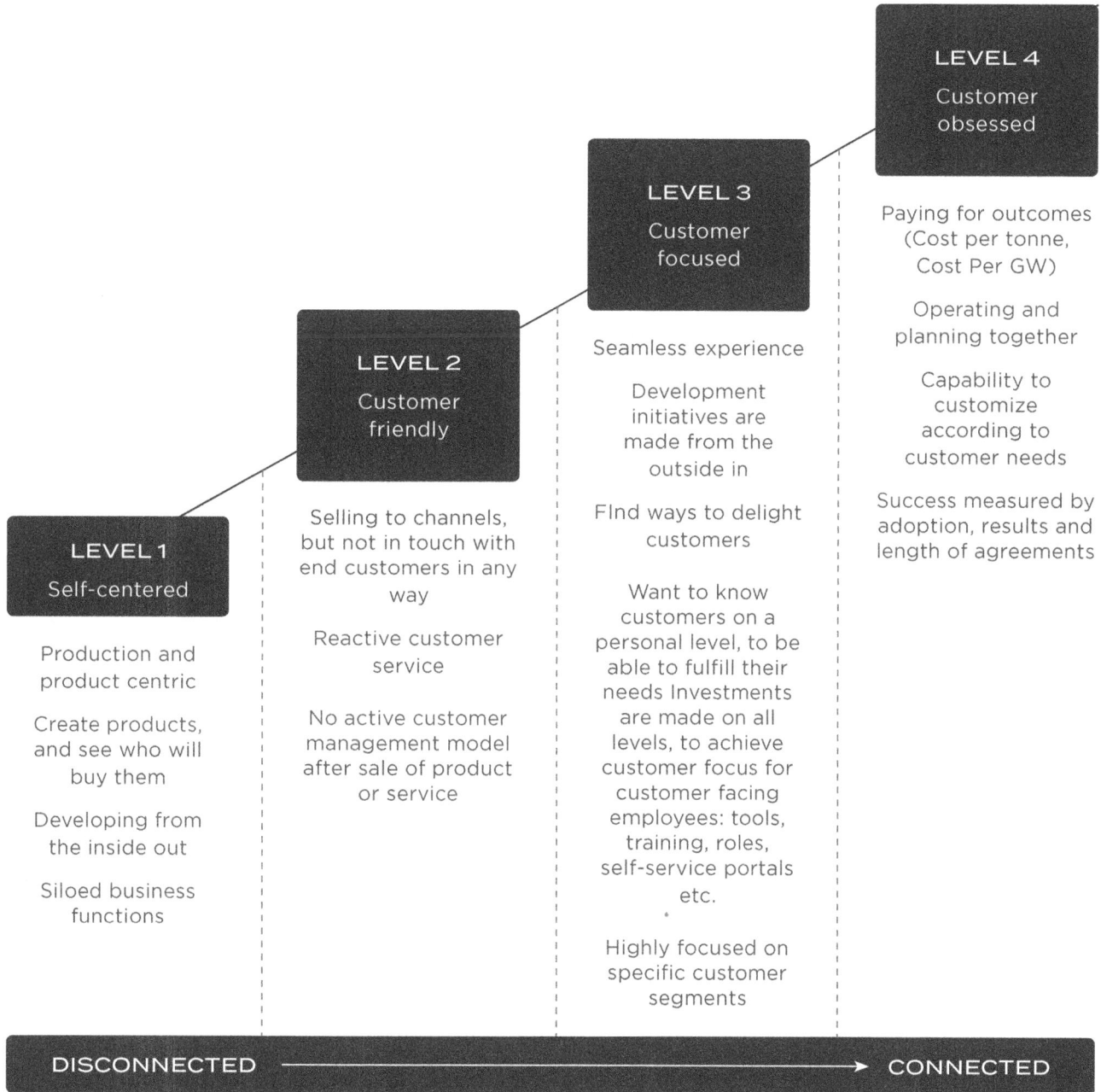

LEVEL 4
Customer obsessed

Paying for outcomes (Cost per tonne, Cost Per GW)

Operating and planning together

Capability to customize according to customer needs

Success measured by adoption, results and length of agreements

LEVEL 3
Customer focused

Seamless experience

Development initiatives are made from the outside in

FInd ways to delight customers

Want to know customers on a personal level, to be able to fulfill their needs Investments are made on all levels, to achieve customer focus for customer facing employees: tools, training, roles, self-service portals etc.

Highly focused on specific customer segments

LEVEL 2
Customer friendly

Selling to channels, but not in touch with end customers in any way

Reactive customer service

No active customer management model after sale of product or service

LEVEL 1
Self-centered

Production and product centric

Create products, and see who will buy them

Developing from the inside out

Siloed business functions

DISCONNECTED ⟶ CONNECTED

THE FOUR LEVELS OF CUSTOMER CENTRICITY

Self-centered

Most companies in the industrial era were of this sort. They didn't need to be customer-centric; they just needed to make sure they were producing products efficiently enough and making sure people were aware of them, and that there was a distribution channel for them. Some companies still operate in this way as they still make their plans and calculations based on their factories and supply chain efficiencies, instead of thinking about the customers first.

Customer-friendly

Being friendly does not mean that you are focused on the customer. There is a clear difference. Self-centered people do not connect as well with people around them. They might seem friendly, but are not necessarily genuinely friendly. Customer-centricity is something that all companies agree that they are, but when you open the 'hood of the car', or the hood of the organization in this case, and start observing how things work within the organization, it becomes clear that there are many people and processes that are not customer-centric.

Customer-focused

These companies are focused on their customers' needs and fulfilling them with the utmost speed and precision. They conduct surveys and keep their radars in tune to what customers want in the market. Many excellent companies that sell through channels can be level-3 companies, but no matter what they do they are never fully aligned with their customers' needs as they do not control the customer relationship.

Customer-obsessed

These companies are the Steve Jobses of their industries. They understand their customers' needs so well they can predict what customers will need and drive that need with the insight they have. The difference between level-4 and level-3 is that level-4 companies don't create products for their customers; they create products with their customers. They innovate together, in a way that forms a symbiosis between customer and company. This symbiosis is the same as in biology, where both organisms benefit from each other, and are therefore better off together than apart. Level-4 companies are often not considered to be vendors by their customers, but rather partners or an extension of their own organization in one way or another. At level 4, customers become a part of a community that shares and drives the innovations of the future.

INTERVIEW: MIKKO LEINONEN, HEAD OF CUSTOMER AND SALES SOLUTIONS AT KONE

ABOUT KONE

KONE is a leader in the elevator and escalator industry known for its dedication to 'People Flow'.

YOUR STRATEGY HIGHLIGHTS THE IMPORTANCE OF CUSTOMER EXPERIENCE. HOW DO YOU DEFINE CUSTOMER EXPERIENCE?

Customer experience is the sum of all the interactions with the customer along their journey. Understanding both the heart and more rational mind are very important. With this I mean the emotional part of the customer's journey as well as how they are interacting with us across all the different channels.

WHY SHOULD THE C-LEVEL BE INTERESTED IN CUSTOMER EXPERIENCE?

It's the competitive advantage of the future. Of course, efficiency and product offering are still important, and depending on the company strategy these must be at a satisfactory or excellent level, but what clearly differentiates companies from each other in the eyes of the customer will be more and more the experience they provide them.

"I believe that customer experience will become the main reason why customers choose to do business with one company instead of another."

YOUR STRATEGY IS 'WINNING WITH CUSTOMERS'. WHAT DOES THIS MEAN IN PRACTICE?

For over the last ten years our customers have been at the core of our strategy and customer loyalty has been a strategic target for KONE. More than ten years ago customer focus was a strategic development program at KONE. Then in 2011 customer experience was taken up as a strategic initiative. This was way before 'CX' (customer experience) was a buzzword like it is today, so KONE was already one step ahead by talking about customer experience seven years ago. It's natural to take the next step to go even deeper, and the most suitable way to describe this renewed focus is: Winning with customers.

This added customer focus is very important because both customers and the users of our solutions are more demanding and powerful than ever before. The experience we are providing our customers in all touchpoints is the key part of our value proposition and the competitive edge we have over our competitors.

If we want to succeed in the age of the customer, we must alter our thinking. We need to think even more from the outside in. This means we need to help our customers become more successful. Instead of thinking about our own success, we are now thinking one step further.

If we go deeper into the topic of winning with customers, I think it's about creating a differentiated experience that is either about the ease of using a solution, or buying it, or always being able to have a 'wow' impact – so a differentiated experience. At KONE we are thinking about the whole customer lifecycle and everything that can happen during the journey that could be, let's say, 70 years together.

To bring our strategy to life, we have introduced four Ways to Win, with our customers which are:

- *Collaborative innovation and new competences; for example, how we innovate together with customers and users and introduce new services quickly.*

- *Customer-centric solutions and services; for example, by working closely and broadly with different customers and proactively finding the best match for their individual needs.*

- *Fast and smart execution; by this we mean increasing speed and working smarter to focus on activities that are valuable to the customer.*

- *True service mindset; this means taking ownership of delivering what is important to your customers and colleagues.*

So now we are putting the customer in the center, and then we think about our products, services and processes. It's a mindset change in how we develop everything at the company.

HOW DO YOU MEASURE THE JOURNEYS?

We do have a traditional annual relationship questionnaire. But more and more we are putting weight on customer feedback after key moments, such as a service visit. We want to get data to support the different parts of the journey, and then compare this to business metrics to find correlations and improvement opportunities.

WHAT IS THE ROLE OF TECHNOLOGY IN DEVELOPING CUSTOMER EXPERIENCE?

It has been an enabler before, but slowly technology is becoming a driver of change. A good example would be the role of platforms. Salesforce CRM at KONE starting from 2006 was the enabler for sales. The CRM for us is also digital marketing, customer service, analytics and artificial intelligence in both decision-making and message personalization. All these things are opening new opportunities. Earlier you had to be truly visionary to do great things with technology in sales. At the same time, to get the basics in place for the supply chain, you 'just' had to choose a platform like SAP and you could streamline the whole process and then start building additional capabilities and innovations. For sales, service and marketing you had to go extra miles to be able to piece everything together. I think the same thing that happened to streamlining the supply chain with SAP, has now happened when you choose a platform like Salesforce. Instead of having to be very visionary, you can just choose a platform and choose which capabilities you want to start using and think how you can change your business to operate according to best practices, so from this angle I see technology as a driver of change, because the barriers to using it are becoming so low.

Additionally, up until now digitizing sales has been hard compared to digitizing financial and production processes, but now the same process development mentality has shifted over to sales and marketing.

However, to be fair, at the same time there have been thousands of innovative solutions for certain sales and marketing technology areas like advertising or analytics. This means that if you constantly want to stay in front of the competition, you must be aware of new innovations and development.

See more about this in Chapter 11 – Technology components of your Growth Platform

ARE ALL YOUR PRODUCT AND SERVICES PRICED TRADITIONALLY OR DO YOU HAVE OUTCOME- OR SUBSCRIPTION-BASED MODELS?

We do not have truly outcome-based solutions yet, but of course we are thinking about new business models. As of now we have our 24/7 Connected Services, which is used for example for predictive maintenance and charged based on a monthly fee. It has all the elements to be developed towards an outcome-based model. We also have a range of digital services enhancing the experience of end users such as KONE Residential Flow offering, launched in 2017, which helps customers in our residential segment as they can use applications for example to open doors and see who is at their door conveniently from their mobile device. These types of applications will be new services that we are launching with subscription models. These types of applications will change the world and the industry's business models along with it.

WHAT DO YOU THINK SHOULD BE AUTOMATED AND WHAT NEEDS A HUMAN TOUCH?

The thing that we should be thinking about is, how could marketing, sales and other interactions be automated so that the customer can do as much as possible themselves and how can marketing be automated to augment what sales people have done before. Digitalization enables customers to do much more themselves, when it comes to simple or well-packaged solutions, and with, for example, intuitive sales configurators customers can do a big part of their buying process. Sales people should therefore focus on specific customer segments and solutions, that would otherwise not be buying if someone wasn't consultatively selling to them.

See more about Chapter 7 –
What should be automated?

HOW DO SALES, SERVICE AND MARKETING COOPERATE AT KONE?

We have succeeded because we have given more power and responsibility to the front lines to make decisions that impact customers. That's one thing. The other is that we've been mapping customer journeys together. Three different business lines have been building their customer journeys. They all have their own customer segments, and the three businesses do not have the same customer journey so it made sense to look at this separately. But from a holistic perspective, on a high level,

we look at them as one joint customer experience. The customer journeys help marketing, sales and service understand each other's KPIs and what the joint responsibilities are in progressing customers in the journey. These customer journeys, KPIs and descriptions of the joint responsibilities help the different departments cooperate.

See more about this in Chapter 9 –
Re-designing roles to support the customer journey and Chapter 10 – Marketing and customer success become crucial

WHAT IS YOUR ADVICE TO COMPANIES THAT WANT TO MODERNIZE THE WAY THEY SELL?

First, understand your own services, your customer segments, the buying behavior and the market logic. Create a few different key categories, so that you can clearly differentiate what types of different sales models you should have. This will give a good view of what should and could be automated and what still needs humans. This exercise should give you answers to questions like: should buying your solutions be automated/self-service or will traditional field sales still be responsible? Should customers have self-service configurators to build their own solutions and then complete their purchase? When you look at the cooperation of sales and marketing, before it was about marketing softening the beach, and sales going in after this to close and get the glory. But now with digital marketing you can sell, so that sales people do not even need to be in the field for marketing to create sales. But all this of course depends on what you sell. All these opportunities are easy to evaluate when you start by analyzing your different customer segments and gradually move towards a 'segment of one' and greater personalization.

See more about this in Chapter 9 –
Re-designing roles to support the customer journey

HOW HAS SALES CHANGED AND WHERE IS SALES HEADING?

The first thing that comes to mind is the increased amount of data we can capture about customers to understand them better. How we then use that data at the point they interact with sales has changed the game because it enables a much more personalized buying experience. This means that the way selling is done must also change. The amount of manual labor that sales has done before will be reduced and sales people will focus on tasks that require more emotional intelligence and creativity. Automation is now replacing many of the normal tasks in the beginning and end of the traditional sales process. I also see that since pricing has become so transparent, the role of sales people has changed. Sales people are more responsible than ever to make sure that all interactions with customers are positive and that they are adding value, whether the interactions lead to a won deal or not.

With data we are also going more towards this 'segment of one'. So instead of working with large broad segments, soon we can personalize all communications and interactions with customers no matter what channel or person is talking to the customer. When marketing becomes this targeted, the tasks of sales people will be focused on even higher value than before.

See more about this in Chapter 9 –
Re-designing roles to support the customer journey

HOW HAS MARKETING AUTOMATION CHANGED SALES?

It is forcing sales people to be more productive and focus on higher-value activities. To start with, we have a combination of people and tools that are qualifying leads and working on them before handing over to sales. In certain cases, the person qualifying the leads can even create small offers for sales people for closing. This frees up the time of sales people so they can focus on activity with the highest value and impact, which means spending time with the right customers and selling instead of doing something else.

See more about this in Chapter 9 –
Re-designing roles to support the customer journey and Chapter 10 – Marketing and customer success become crucial.

Now we have explored the major forces that are changing B2B businesses. Business models are shifting to subscriptions and outcomes, and customer experience is becoming the main way to differentiate. Companies need to shift focus from manufacturing and selling products, to helping customers become successful. Whether you have a subscription business model, a traditional business model or a combination of both, the pressure from the modern customer is forcing you to build an organization and processes that are more in line with how customers want to buy.

In the next chapters we take the first steps towards building a Growth Platform. We'll look at the typical stages of a customer's lifecycle, and share some thoughts around segmentation. These are the first steps before putting the right organization and technology in place.

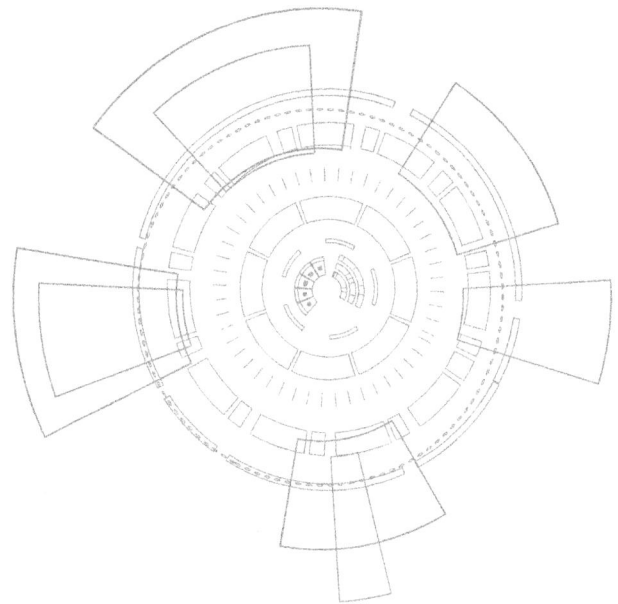

PART II

IMPLEMENTING A GROWTH PLATFORM

CHAPTER 5

/ THE CUSTOMER LIFECYCLE

Customers are empowered and they demand faster service from the companies whose products and services they purchase. At the same time, many customers are happier to subscribe to what they need, rather than buying products. To be successful in meeting the demands of the modern customer and achieving growth, companies must become more connected through the customer's entire lifecycle and split it into different stages. Being able to focus on specific parts of the customer's lifecycle leads to a more scalable organization that can react and improve the quality of customer engagement.

Whether a company is shifting towards an outcome-based offering or focusing on just maximizing results with the current offering, becoming connected to their customers means they will be able to take better care of customers during their whole lifecycle. Focusing on specific stages of the customer's lifecycle instead of short-term transactions, leads to longer and healthier customer relationships and a sales, marketing and service organization that can be scaled; so growth is easier to achieve.

All of this, however, increases the touchpoints and complexity of doing business, but this is exactly the complexity that IT systems are designed to help with. Luckily, information technology like customer relationship management systems (CRM), marketing automation, self-serve portals, IoT and e-commerce now makes it easier for companies to excel both in changing their business model and developing customer relationship management.

THE LIFECYCLE BECOMES MORE IMPORTANT WHEN COMPETING ON CUSTOMER EXPERIENCE

There are many ways to compete in business, but competing on products alone is becoming increasingly difficult, because products and services that were once unique, have now become commoditized, which means customers cannot tell products and services apart.

Because of this, many companies are betting their investments on customer experience, to gain a competitive advantage in the market. Understanding the importance of customer experience and acting accordingly are, however, two separate things. In a previous chapter, we presented a statistic that 72% of companies say that improving customer experience is a top priority. Even though many companies claim to operate customer-centrically, words are not backed up by actions, as this IMD study shows. IMD surveyed 454 executives and this is what they found:

Almost 63% of executives said that understanding customers and acting on that understanding was critical to success. However, when it came to business practice, just 24% told them that they had a customer-led approach to running their company. [*]

The rest of the chapters in this book focus on how to build a customer-centric organization that can deliver a customer experience that gives a competitive advantage.

If the goal is to improve customer experience, this means that customer management will become critical and investing only in CRM technology will not be sufficient. The whole operating model from roles, processes, technology and management will need changing from the current way of doing things.

Before putting all the necessary building blocks in place to have a customer-centric operating model, there are a few critical questions we will need to answer, which are: what do the best customers look like? What are bad customers for us? What is the optimal customer lifecycle? Understanding customers and how we want the relationship to develop will help us build everything we need to steer them through the different stages.

MODELING THE CUSTOMER LIFECYCLE

Depending on the business model, the customer lifecycle will have different levels of importance and different stages. As competition gets tougher in most industries, the cost of customer acquisition will increase, and the focus on retaining customers will become increasingly important. Choosing customers more carefully and having a long-term point of view is key. For this reason, the customer lifecycle depicted here has a short new business acquisition phase and a longer retain and grow phase.

This is a visual representation of a typical customer lifecycle. The key point is that instead of thinking about the customer relationship as transactional or just a typical funnel, we look at it from the perspective of a long-term relationship.

CUSTOMER LIFECYCLE STAGES

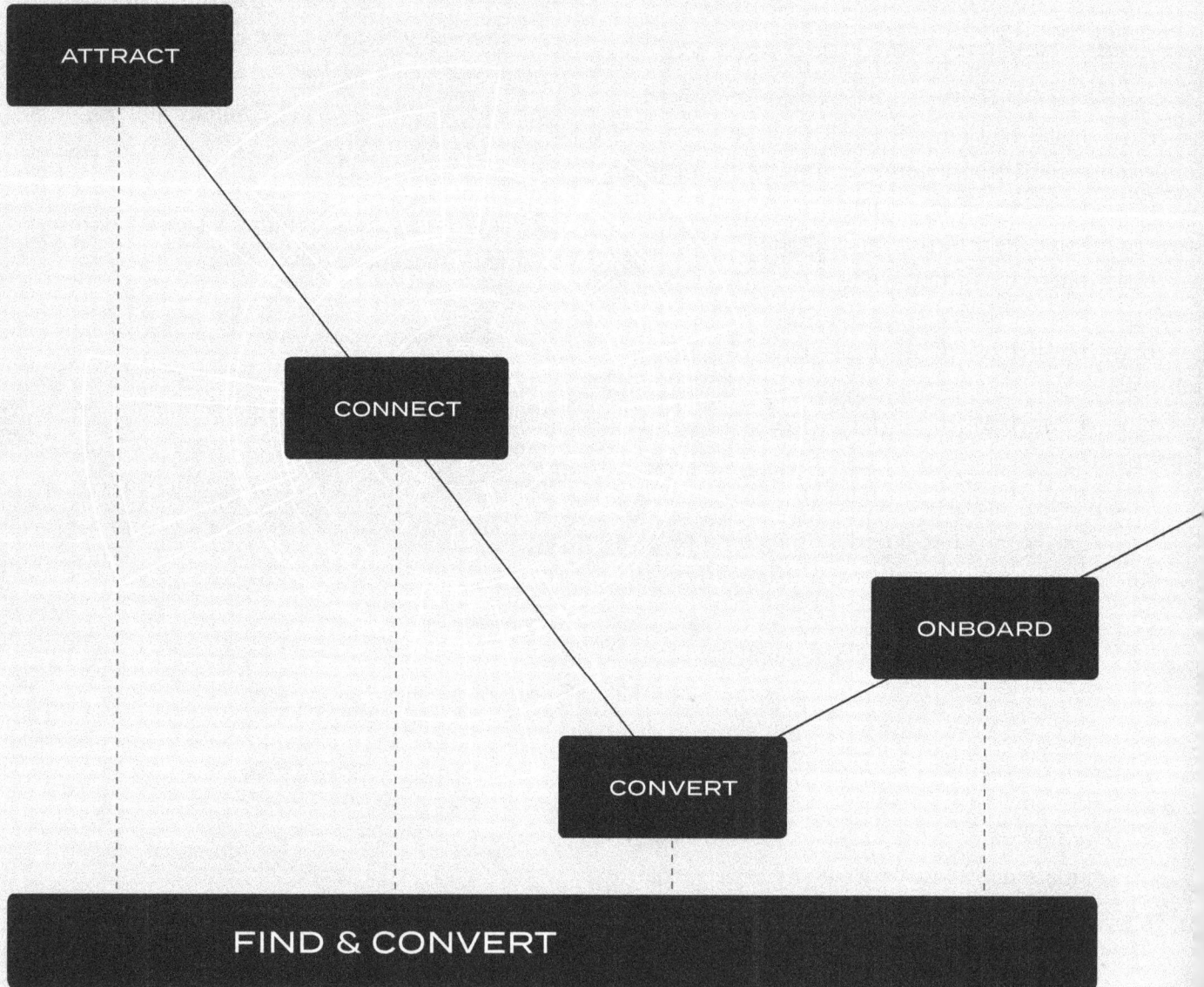

ATTRACT

CONNECT

ONBOARD

CONVERT

FIND & CONVERT

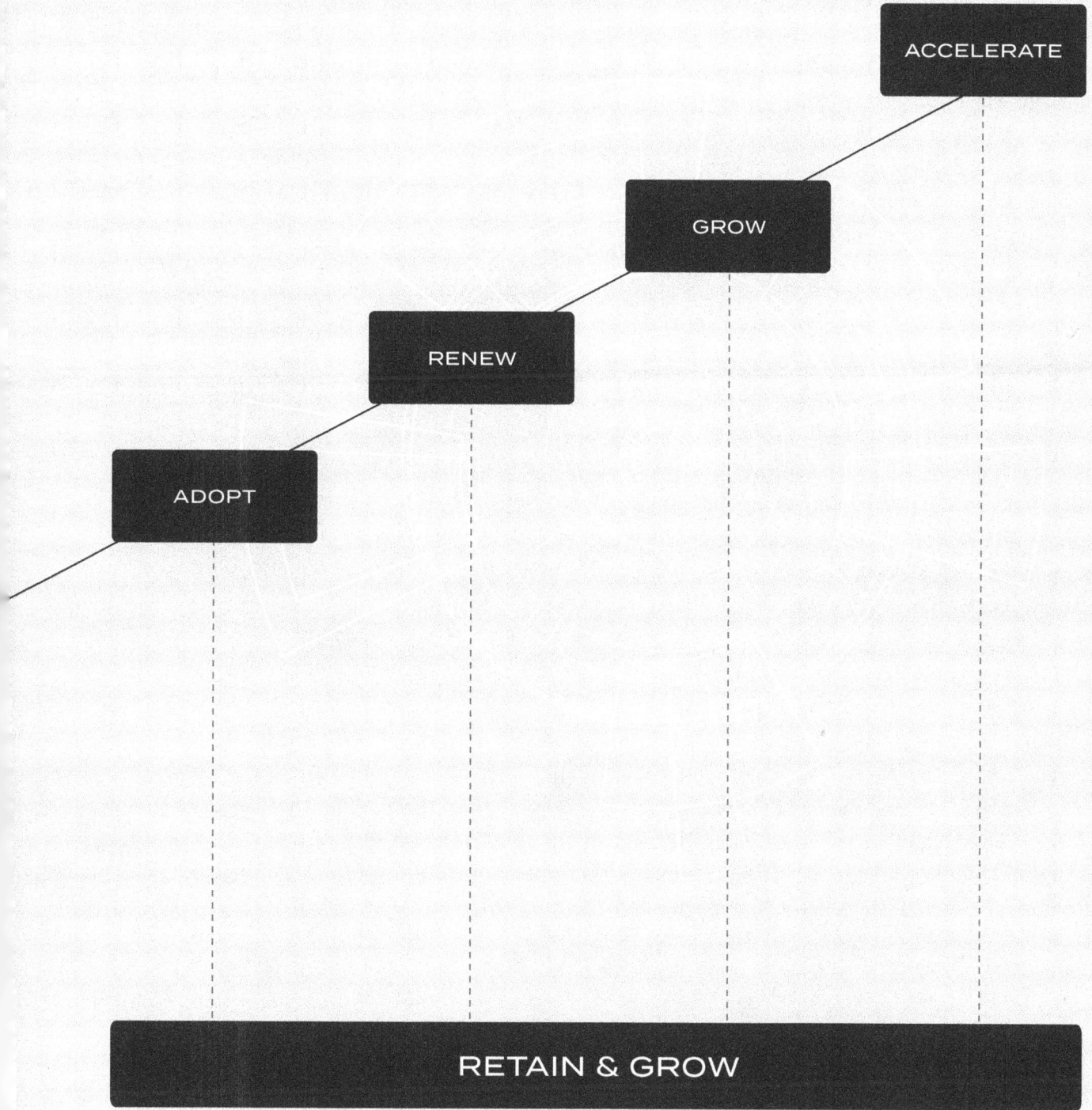

ACCELERATE

GROW

RENEW

ADOPT

RETAIN & GROW

STEERING THE RELATIONSHIP FROM PROSPECT TO STRATEGIC ACCOUNT

Knowing which customers should develop into strategic accounts should already be clear before the attract phase, because you need to have a way of calculating how much you are willing to invest in finding and converting prospect to customers. Acquiring new customers will keep getting tougher all the time, which means it will get more expensive. Homing in on the best customers, with a long potential journey together is key. You must choose customers more carefully than before. With some customers you may just want to offer the most basic product or service, while with others you may have very large up-selling and cross-selling opportunities. Taking a longer view on the customer relationship puts more focus on customer acquisition.

The further a customer progresses in the stages in the lifecycle, the more connected the vendor becomes with the customer. This means that barriers to competitors increase as you progress further along the lifecycle. The more connected you are with your customers, the faster you can react to problems and issues that need to be corrected. The more connected you are with your customer, the more value you can create for them.

The lifecycle model can also be used for sales planning for large strategic account selling. If a sales executive has five accounts he/she is working on, he/she can use these stages to identify where the customers are and what they have the potential of developing into. One customer could be a fresh one that has just been signed a few months ago, which is still in the onboarding stage. One customer has been a customer for a couple years and has potential to grow, but they have only renewed the original contract so far. The sales executive is figuring out how to move that specific account from only being a renew customer, to getting them to the growth stage. The sales executive also has one strategic account, which is the most valuable account. Then there is one prospect to be contacted this quarter which has the potential to become a strategic customer. Additionally, there is one prospect in the convert stage with negotiations ongoing right now.

Here are some examples of typical things that happen in the different lifecycle stages.

CUSTOMER LIFECYCLE STAGES

FIND & CONVERT

ATTRACT

The attract phase is when the prospects attention is directed towards the company and the value it could be creating for them. It could be through traditional advertising, or some kind of content online. It could also be that the person is searching for a solution to a problem and stumble upon a search results that leads to your website or a Google ad you have placed for certain keywords. Word of mouth whether in the traditional sense, or online is also a normal thing that happens in this stage. Attracting could also be done by business development representatives for accounts with enough potential value.

CONNECT

If you have been able to get the customers attention and enough trust in the attract phase, then you will have a much easier time to succeed in the connect phase. Connecting can happen in a numerous amount of ways such as with a chatbot, email, phone, face to face, online meeting. There are many ways to connect and it could also be completely automated depending on how easy it is for customers to engage with you.

CONVERT

This stage is critical no matter what business you are in. A converting customer can mean a 50 $/month contract or 500,000 deal that a sales executive has been working on for months or years, so the amount of work it takes to convert a customer will be radically different. For some companies there can be many conversions. First a trial conversion and then the customer converts to a paying customer, which means that this convert stage could have several steps before a customer converts to a paying customer.

RETAIN & GROW

ONBOARD

In the onboarding stage we make sure we deliver on what was promised. If the customer does not get the promised value out of what they have bought then they will not buy anymore, even if it was their own fault they weren't able to get the value they were hoping for. If they feel that the vendor has not delivered on what they promised then they will not work with them any longer.

Strive to have a 'wow' effect in this stage and you're off to a long profitable relationship.

ADOPT

In the adopt phase, the key is to make sure everyone that can benefit from the product or service begins to benefit according to the plan or what has been promised. Onboarding was a short and efficient stage, while adoption is a continuous stage that lasts for the whole lifecycle of the specific product. The product in use may change and develop over time and so will the customer's situation, so it is important to continuously ensure correct and valuable adoption.

RENEW

Ensure that the contract is renewed. For many, this is an opportunity to build and integrate with the next phase which is Grow. When the customer is satisfied with what they currently have, we have a good chance to not only renew the current contract, but change the content of the contract to fulfill even more of the customer's needs. There is no reason to wait to grow the relationship until the renew phase. The point however is that if you cannot renew the first contract, or you have a difficult time in renewing it, then it will be difficult to grow.

GROW

The more value you create for a customer the more you can potentially grow the relationship. Many use a whitespace analysis to understand what additional areas they could help customers in. This is something that should already be done in the customer acquisition phase to ensure that the most valuable customers are acquired. Most companies have a 'land and expand strategy' and for those this is the most crucial phase of them all.

ACCELERATE

The goal for customers that have a strategic significance is a symbiotic relationship, meaning that as the relationship progresses and deepens, both parties will experience increased benefit. The only way to deepen the relationship is to learn from each other and form a type of symbiotic relationship.

The goal is to become the key partner to the customer in your scope of expertise. There should be significant benefits from expanding the relationship to this level. By investing in the relationship, both parties should get the most out of it. This is, of course, where segmenting comes into play, as you cannot and do not want to accelerate all customers to a strategic level.

CHAPTER 6

/ CUSTOMER SEGMENTATION

The customer lifecycle model presented in the last chapter was generic, so it works in any industry for mapping how to steer customers. In this chapter with customer segmentation we will need to get more specific than the lifecycle. In the context of this book we will look at customer segmentation as a strategic decision about which customers to focus on. Segmentation is a strategic decision, because it takes a stance on how a B2B company will allocate its resources. Understanding which customers will get more attention and focus, and which will not, leads us to how the account management model will be built. Segmentation can be done on a much deeper and more advanced level than ever before thanks to a multitude of different technologies, but here we will just maintain a high-level account tier segmentation.

Depending on the value and potential value of a customer, there will be different ways we will want to guide them through the different lifecycle stages portrayed in chapter 5. What dictates how the customer is guided throughout the lifecycle is what type of customer segment they belong to. Some customers will be worth hundreds of millions, some millions, others may only be worth thousands through their lifetime. Some will be continuous transactions of thousands of orders per year while others may only have a few upgrades during their lifetime. The approach to maximizing the value of the relationship will happen very differently depending on the potential. In this chapter we will keep the topic of segmentation short and simple, by splitting customers into different tiers based on value.

SEGMENTING THROUGH DEEPER LIFECYCLE UNDERSTANDING

Some customers are willing to pay much more than others for the same products and services. If there is a serious need, then of course the customer will be willing to pay more. Just like if a person is stuck in the desert thirsty, the willingness to pay more for water will be much higher than at home with fresh drinking water in the fridge. It's exactly the same product, but a completely different customer in two completely different situations.

Understanding that willingness to pay changes so much from one company to another, it shouldn't come as a surprise that many companies' customer bases are built on the pareto principle. That means that 20% of customers bring in 80% of revenue. The pareto effect is true for volume and revenue, but for many it will be shocking to know that the profit of 20% of customers might be bringing in over 100% of final profits. Wait, how could it be over 100%? The reason for this is that many customers that companies take care of are actually unprofitable as they are taking up valuable resources without being high value customers.

It's good to fully understand that there are wide differences in the profitability of customers, which should impact how different accounts are managed. Unfortunately, many companies manage different customers with a broadly similar account management model. If this is the case, then many customers that are paying more or would be willing to pay more, are getting as much attention as lower-value customers that may even be using up more resources in customer support. These low-value customers should either be put on a self-serve model, or just let go of completely. It is wrong not to have a customer management model split up by value and profit, because the customers that are willing to pay for your prices without always complaining and who do not take up your resources deserve your attention more than customers who take up your resources without being as valuable. When customer support is handed over to all customers requesting it, then higher-value customers may not be getting the attention they deserve.

CALCULATING CUSTOMER LIFETIME VALUE

Calculating and estimating customer lifecycle value is a must for creating your segments, so that you can allocate resources properly and build suitable customer journeys for each segment.
In Chapter 9 – Re-designing roles to support the customer journey, there will be more detailed descriptions about how to build roles by segment.

How much value can you create?

Instead of asking how much revenue you can potentially get from a specific customer before putting them into a specific customer tier, what if we would ask how much value we can create for them? Approaching segmenting by the value you can create is more natural and customer-centric and leads to better insights and focus. The more value you can create for customers with your products and services, the more they can buy from you, so it makes sense to put more resources into the top tiers.

If a customer has the potential to be a high-tier A customer, then they should be managed the same way as an A customer is managed, even though they may be a C customer from a current revenue generation perspective.

Here is a sample of the different customer tiers divided by the different levels according to potential total sales or current sales.

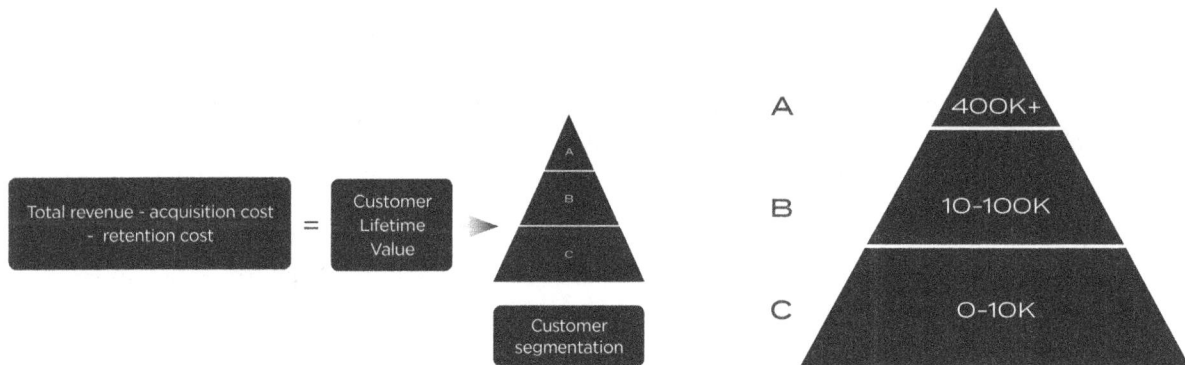

In the next chapter we'll take a closer look at the various approaches to managing different customers segments.

Next we have the interview with Johnson Controls' former CMO, Kim Metcalf-Kupres. She highlights the benefits of segmentation for building the right approach to sales and marketing. In the interview you'll also get brilliant insights on topics such as CRM implementation and change management.

INTERVIEW: KIM METCALF-KUPRES, FORMER VP AND CMO OF JOHNSON CONTROLS

ABOUT KIM METCALF-KUPRES

Kim is the former VP and CMO of Johnson Controls. As CMO, Metcalf-Kupres led the full spectrum of marketing functions for the company, including strategy, innovation, product management, sales and communications. In this role, she was responsible for directing strategies, capabilities and major initiatives designed to drive profitable growth, delivering new ways of creating value for customers and building the company's brand.

HOW DO YOU SEE THAT SALES AND MARKETING HAS CHANGED IN THE LAST 20 YEARS AND WHY?

The most dramatic changes go hand in hand with the bigger changes in society and the way people live. Our own experiences as consumers have changed our expectations as professionals. Our expectations around speed, quality, and the ease of getting information has forever changed purchasing both in transactional B2B business as well as more complex B2B sales. All this comes down to the customer being able to get informa-tion themselves, which has dramatically reduced the need to rely on sales people for information. What you see is that the whole buying process has changed and buyers' criteria becomes more and more specific all the time. People are much more aware and they are less afraid and they are more confident about their own ability to educate themselves. Their willingness and ability to experiment with change and the low cost of switching to try other products or services is making it increasingly difficult to hold on to customers. It's not enough to get back to someone within a week, you have to get back to them within an hour or even minutes. The expectations both for responsiveness and the quality of responding to customers is incredibly different from before.

WHAT HAS NOT CHANGED?

What is the same is the importance of relationships. I don't mean sales people golfing with customers, I mean people who are the best at long-term relationships that focus on helping customers accomplish their goals. The sales people and account teams that are the most successful are those who are really close to their customers and focused on helping other people succeed. If you can leverage the technology available today to scale how you help customers, then you have a winning approach. People do need the human factor and creativity that automation and the internet cannot provide.

WHAT PROBLEMS WILL A COMPANY FACE IF SALES AND MARKETING ARE NOT ALIGNED?

There are a lot of symptoms and things you can usually observe when sales and marketing within a company are not aligned. Firstly, you have confused and unsatisfied customers. Even if you maintain these customers they can be characterized as being trapped, because of high switching costs – as one example. The symptoms will be organizations going after the wrong customers that aren't valuable or profitable. These could be very large customers with scale that may seem attractive because of volume but you may be losing money on them. It's the reason I emphasize the importance of understanding who your best customers are, having clarity about the company strategy and then really putting discipline in place to stick to the overall plan.

In a complex solutions-oriented environment there will also be difficulty competing if sales and marketing are not aligned, because the linkages between brand, awareness, consideration and engagement will be weak. As a result, you will more likely be involved late in the buying cycle as opposed to shaping and influencing the specifications. In this case you will end up answering to specs driven by your competitors.

Misalignment also leads to poor product development pipelines and inefficient product launches.

Sales engagement is one of the best ways to ensure good access to the 'voice of the customer' input needed for quality feedback and identifying new or emerging opportunities. At the other end of the process, even though you may have a great product and a good promotional plan, your product launch will still be unsuccessful if the salesforce is not ready to sell it yet. So, misalignment also leads to slow product launches that waste time and opportunity.

Without true cooperation between sales and marketing you may also discover a lot of duplicate work which leads to wasted energy and money for the company. People will show up with weird titles like 'technical sales support' or 'product marketing', and in these organizations redundancy occurs because separate teams are trying to fill needs independently that they should be filling together. Rather than having combined and integrated organizations under one roof that seamlessly work together hand in hand, you will get turf battles wherein there will be more people than you need working in a redundant fashion spending money and budgets that could be better used.

See more about this in Chapter 9 –
Re-designing roles to support the customer journey and Chapter 10 – Marketing and customer success become crucial

WHAT ARE A FEW KEYS TO ALIGNING SALES AND MARKETING?

This may seem simple, but often the best advice is the simple fundamental stuff. Start with the customer first and design everything with the customer experience at the center. Starting with the customer, and then combining this understanding with your strategy and your performance objectives are crucial steps to marketing and sales alignment. Answering these types of questions will guide your alignment initiatives: What defines success for your company? What are you good at? How do you maintain a competitive advantage? Are you a growth company or not? Are you trying to disrupt or are you trying to optimize?

WHAT ARE SOME EXAMPLES OF JOINT METRICS FOR SALES AND MARKETING TO LOOK AT?

There are a few key things every good commercial metric system should capture. At Johnson Controls we built our whole customer satisfaction system around multiple points of measurement in order to balance both point in time with ongoing feedback. We were doing inquiry and surveying on a quite continuous basis. We found that in most of our long-term business-to-business segments 'customer loyalty' was the best measure, particularly for large strategic accounts. This metric was obtained through a standardized process and a disciplined survey methodology

that was applied consistently across the organization and integrated into our CRM system. In our more transactional businesses, simple real-time measures of immediate experience such as net promoter score were more relevant. The key for every organization is to understand the dynamics of the customer's experience, the scope of the relevant interactions across the firm and tie metrics as tightly to these as possible. The most common mistake with surveys is asking the wrong people the wrong questions at the wrong time. Understand your customer and design your measuring system to avoid these easy pitfalls.

The other essential measurements of marketing and sales effectiveness are health metrics that give an end-to-end view of the processes from awareness and consideration through pipeline cultivation, engagement and conversion that are critical to commercial performance. The organization must know how much pipeline is needed to support its business objectives in all stages of the funnel, from the early phases down to negotiation and winning deals. It's particularly important to have a clear understanding of these process components and associated metrics before trying to implement any marketing automation or e-commerce platforms.

So, combining the continuous feedback and balancing this with pipeline health and conversion

are the keys for alignment. If you are only meas-
uring sales productivity and hit-rate, those num-
bers are easy to game by reducing the number of
sales people, or reducing opportunities that are
pursued. If you do that you feel good for a bit,
but you are serving a smaller and smaller piece
of the market.

Some things are harder to measure than others,
but all activities should in one way or another be
tied to customer satisfaction and building enough
pipeline to reach targets.

See more about this in Chapter 10 –
Marketing and customer success become crucial

WITH THE ADVENT OF E-COMMERCE, DO YOU THINK MARKETING AND CUSTOMER SERVICE SHOULD OWN SOME SEGMENTS THAT DO NOT REQUIRE THE ATTENTION OF SALES EXECUTIVES?

This really raises a philosophical dialogue around
what selling is? How do you define a sale or
selling? Usually many assume that selling always
involves a direct force of people, and that is be-
coming less and less the case.

Nobody at the gas station helps you pump your
gas any longer. At retail stores you go in already
knowing what you want, you pick it out, pay

through an automated checkout and off you go.
The more complicated the purchase, of course,
the harder it is to disrupt the way 'sales' is done.
This is because not all buying circumstances are
the same and that's why I'm a big fan of a seg-
mented approach. I'm a believer of segmented
sales processes based on who the customers are,
what they need, the way they want to engage, the
way they want to buy and how the whole deci-
sion-making process is envisioned and executed.

With segmented channel strategies, you end up
with a hybrid sales organization that can serve
different needs. There's no need to assume that
a sales organization becomes obsolete, because
with such a strategy it doesn't mean that a tra-
ditional marketing organization can just take
over. You can't just stop at the awareness and
consideration part of the buying process. There
must be some effective means to shepherd the
engagement, selection and transaction elements
that ultimately get the customer to complete a
purchase. The more difficult the solution set or
the buying process, the more difficult this is to
replicate through automation alone.

Now that customers have become so inde-
pendent, the ownership of the sales funnel and
function has changed. Ownership of the sale
could be in the marketing function and it could
just be called the commercial organization. I've

seen the commercial responsibility also sitting in operations in some of the tech companies. For example, at Facebook Sheryl Sandberg the COO owns the sales funnel and sales responsibility. Sometimes even the IT department can have ownership of sales, but that can be a bit risky because traditional IT professionals have focused on the technology and not so much on the customers.

I think we are going to see organizations become much more dynamic in relation to who has ownership of managing customers. The specifics will vary by organization and industry, however, the most important theme of customer-centricity and connection will endure regardless of where that ownership resides.

See more about this in Chapter 6 – Customer segmentation and Chapter 9 – Re-designing roles to support the customer journey

WHAT ARE THE CORRECT STEPS TO TAKE WHEN IMPLEMENTING A NEW CRM OR MARKETING AUTOMATION TECHNOLOGY?

One of the worst things you can do is invest in technology for technology's sake. So, as Stephen Covey so wisely advised, start with the end in mind and be very clear about the objective and your definition of success. If you are trying to eliminate the salesforce as opposed to enabling the salesforce with a CRM system, these are going to be two different things with two very different solutions. It's also important that there is clear context for overall business intelligence, data management and integration for the enterprise across individual systems. Without clarity on where the whole business wants to go, it becomes very hard to integrate the different needs and develop your marketing and sales technology in a way that is not dysfunctional and costly.

Once you have a high-level strategy, then you need to outline your priorities for technology that will help you get there. After articulating your objectives, the next step is to outline the details of current business processes and determine how a new technology will either replace or alter the existing model so that critical things get done better, faster and/or cheaper.

One problem that many companies have faced is that they often implement a CRM application that doesn't fully appreciate the details of the life of a sales person. When that happens, the chance of organ rejection and dismissal goes up radically.

I think, however, that implementing technology has become easier now with the generational change in talent. Over the last 20 years the willingness to use technology has changed. Not only are current generations of sales professionals more open and willing to use technology, they expect to use technology and they expect to have tools that will ensure they succeed at their jobs. So, I think the obstacles that we were facing earlier with CRM adoption are fading away and that is a good thing. But, these days it's even more important that you enlist people before implementing new technology because everyone is more tech-savvy with higher expectations and good insights that can be applied to making systems even more valuable.

At the same time as the willingness to use technology has increased, the expectations of all the users has also increased. It's got to be super easy and fast to use and the worst thing that happens is taking people away from time with customers and spending their time on rudimentary and repetitive data entry tasks. Companies like Salesforce and others have made these obstacles almost non-existent, because the tools are so much more consistent with the tools and apps we use as individual consumers.

So, the technology we use needs to be super easy and fast to use, and this brings us to the integration requirements topic. How is data shared across the organization and how are the different systems being used? You don't want different systems in marketing creating leads that need to be input in a different way on the sales side, because you want your access to customer information over time to be easily harvested so you can see the value of an account, trends over time, trends in pricing, segment-specific data by product lines or geographical areas.

We now have an enormous opportunity to capture data from so many sources and use that data in all parts of the business, but this means we must have a holistic mindset and great cross-functional engagement.

See more about this in Chapter 11 – Technology components of your Growth Platform

WHAT ARE YOUR TIPS FOR HOW LEADERS SHOULD DRIVE CHANGE?

You must be willing to ask hard questions; not just the questions that make you feel good. Start with your customers and back up your thinking with data. When you know what you need to do, commit fully. You've really got to commit to the change. Burning boats on the shore, as a colleague of mine used to say, is necessary for a full commitment.

People will wait you out, so if you do not fully commit, you will fail.

To be a successful leader you need to be effective with both the formal and the informal ways that things get done in an organization. It doesn't mean you can't switch companies and get off to a quick start when making changes but you have to be able to establish credibility, you have to be respected and you have to build trust. If you are embarking on a major change initiative or building something transformational, it certainly helps to have the relationships and connections in place, so if you are coming into a new organization that's where you really must invest your time, because you need to bring people along with you. If you have terrific ideas, but you're not getting people to support you in the process then you are going to turn around and notice one day that nobody is behind you. The people who are the most successful in their careers take pride in what they do, but they are also very effective at persuading and influencing other people and not pushing everything as their own ideas.

When I look back, really what a leadership or transformational role is about, is sowing seeds that somebody else is going to reap. It means your colleagues are celebrating successes based on foundations you may have put in place three to four years before. Deep down they know that, but you should be able to give them all the credit and let them know this was all their idea. And if you're completely honest with yourself, you'll recognize and admit that much of what you personally have accomplished was built on a foundation you inherited and built via collaboration with others. You cannot get too wound up in your own ego. This means you've got to have strong emotional quotient, not just a high IQ. Change can be hard and especially scary in many organizations. To effectively lead change, your EQ is often more important than your intelligence. This means both understanding the formal and informal ways of working within the company. It requires effective listening with two-way dialogue; frequent, transparent communication; absolute integrity and a dash of humility.

CHAPTER 7

/ WHAT SHOULD BE AUTOMATED?

WHAT SHOULD HUMANS DO AND WHAT SHOULD SYSTEMS DO?

Humans and machines are fundamentally different and both have their strengths and weaknesses, and finding the right balance between humans and machines will be the key to success. The right balance of human and technology will make the business more predictable, scalable and easier to measure, and therefore easier to lead. As we live in the age of the customer in which customer experience creates a competitive advantage, what happens when a company automates something like customer support and it impairs the customer's experience? This is when customers start leaving for competitors. This means the starting point for automating should never be only about lowering costs, but thinking about how technology could help improve the customer experience.

WHAT ARE HUMANS GOOD AT?

So, what are humans good at? For many items outside of what we buy daily such as groceries, buying can be very complex and highly emotional, even for smaller items in B2B. Everyone wants to make a good deal and look good in front of others. The bigger and tougher the decision is, the more important it will be from the seller's side to understand how a person feels and thinks, which will allow them to persuade and influence a customer to make a buying decision. This is especially true for B2B where you could have between 5-15 people involved during the buying process, or on average 6.8 people involved in a purchasing decision.[*]

Each person has their own opinions, needs and goals. A sales executive's role is to be the advisor and help navigate and educate the customer, while being able to identify who is for and who is against them and what their personal motivators are. This would be the emotional intelligence aspect of selling, which is often underrated. In addition to emotional intelligence, the creativity and adaptability of a human being is unlike any machine.

As long as the buying process is complex, it means an account executive will have an important role in planning, coordinating and orchestrating the buying experience, supported by technology and scalable marketing.

WHAT ARE SYSTEMS GOOD AT?

IT systems can do wildly complex problem solving, and never tire. Artificial intelligence can be better and faster at many manual tasks than humans and AI will only keep improving. Artificial intelligence aside, even simple marketing automation does not need any specific intelligence tied to it, just pre-defined customer paths can already

[*] news.cebglobal.com/2016-11-21-Leading-B2B-Sales-Organizations-Challenge-Align-Prescribe-To-Get-Deals-Done

be extremely impactful, generating hundreds of leads per day. This is much more than any person could ever generate.

There are already AI technologies that write emails for sales people, and customers cannot tell whether they are written by humans or AI, because they can be so targeted and well-written. These emails are quite different from the typical template emails, because AI can fetch relevant information online, whether it be articles or news about the company or the exact person that is being contacted. A few companies that are developing technology for this, found with just a quick Google search, were: Nova, Phrasee and Persado. If AI can help write emails that get opened and responded to more often (positively) then heck, why not? You know your competitors are going to be using this technology.

So, it's not such a utopian thought that systems, enhanced by artificial intelligence systems could speak to each other and place orders on their own, without humans intervening.

Since buying is a highly emotional process, and there are many repetitive and manual tasks related to sales, marketing and service then it's very natural to have a clear role for both humans and machines working together. We already see this happening: sales reps are using advanced CRM systems supported by artificial intelligence. Minds and machines complement each other. Every organization should make sure that technology and people are working optimally together. Even though we are talking about technology, that does not mean that we shouldn't be maximizing the human elements of it. By technology we mean customer-facing and internal technology, both powered by artificial intelligence.

INCREASE CUSTOMER ENGAGEMENT WITH TECHNOLOGY

The universal truth about selling has always been, the more you do, the more likely you are to succeed. Want to sell more? Then do more. The activity of a sales executive has always positively correlated with how much they sell, no matter what their skill level is. For highly skilled sales people, even a small level of activity can produce great results, while others must work more. In marketing communications, the same truth holds. The more visibility a brand gets, and the more messaging customers see the better results you will achieve – up to a certain degree where the benefit levels off.

The goal is to be in touch with customers as often as necessary to develop the customer to its fullest potential, but up until now with scarce resources and lack of technologies, it has been very hard to increase interactions, without increasing costs. Just spamming customers with irrelevant messages – as some companies unfortunately do

– is not the right way to increase activity. Once customer segmentation is done, it is easy to make decisions about how technology will support the customer management model for each of the segments. A huge benefit of technology is that, done right, it lowers the costs of customer acquisition and retention.

In complex B2B sales, the way that a sales representative's time and efforts are being focused has changed because of the costs. For example, one face-to-face meeting could cost between 400– 1000 depending on how that is calculated, including working time and travel costs. Each face-to-face meeting must be well prepared, and highly valuable both for the customer and the company for which the sales rep works. With technology it becomes much easier to increase the number of interactions when sales executives are not meeting face-to-face or having an online meeting with customers.

Although costs should not be a driving force in how technology is used to develop customer experience, there should also be cost benefits. Both lowering the cost per interaction and increasing the quality of the interactions is possible with the sales and marketing technology available in the marketplace today. We look closer at these technologies in Chapter 11.

SPLITTING UP THE RESPONSIBILITIES BETWEEN HUMANS AND SYSTEMS

Customer lifetime value should guide all decision making and the use of resources as depicted in the next graph. Along the Y-axis we have the value of the customer over its lifetime and on the X-axis, we have the numbers of customers, or transactions.

Typically, a small business will have a small number of customers and in this case, it will be fine to manage customers manually with human labor. A small company could be running a web shop with thousands of orders per day; in that case it's crucial to cut out all manual processes. The larger the company is and the more transactions and customers there are, the bigger the opportunity is to automate intelligently.

The trick is to maintain the human touch in everything to elevate customer experience, while using automation to streamline and scale with technology where it makes sense for both customers and for the company.

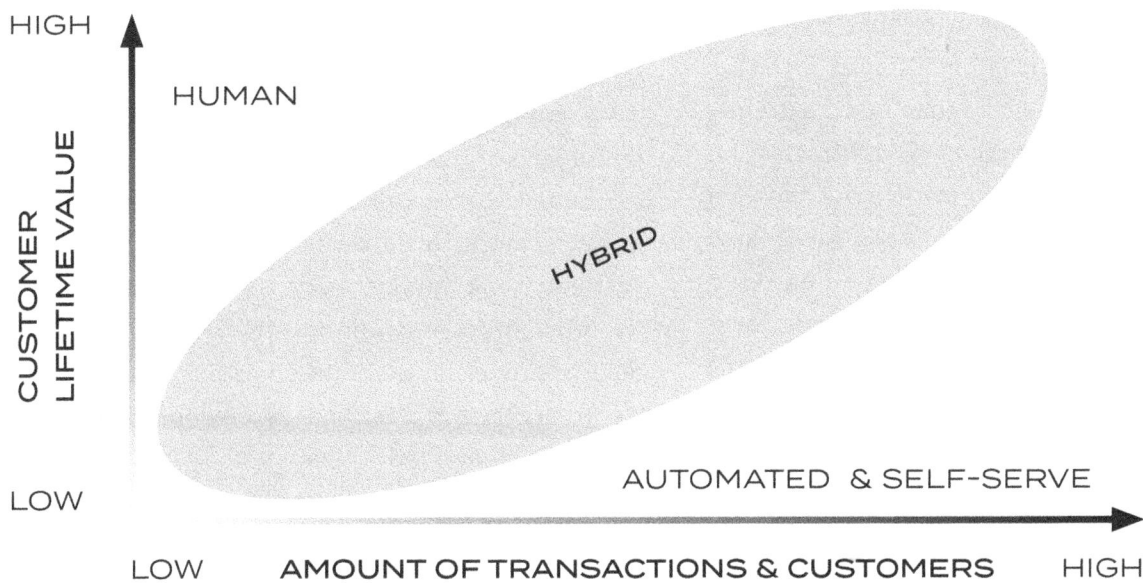

HIGH

HUMAN

CUSTOMER LIFETIME VALUE

HYBRID

AUTOMATED & SELF-SERVE

LOW

LOW   AMOUNT OF TRANSACTIONS & CUSTOMERS   HIGH

HUMAN TOUCH

This is the traditional way of being in touch with customers. Calling, emailing and meeting face-to-face and online.

HYBRID

Using a combination of personal sales and automation/self-serve. Automation is, for example, marketing automation while self-serve would be the customer using some kind of configurator on the vendor's e-commerce website and placing an order.

Since most customers in most B2B companies are managed with the hybrid model, it is not a question of either or, but how to blend both the human touch and automation together. A good example of blending the two together is what Cisco – the networking equipment company – has done. They have built their IT infrastructure in a way so credit can be given to the right people involved in any stage of the sales process, even if the customer orders the products indirectly online, without being directly in touch with the sales person that they talked to at some point.[*]

If a sales person talks to a customer but they are not ready to order yet, and the customer places the order next week online, then the salesperson would also get credit for this. This makes perfect sense, because it shouldn't matter how customers are placing their orders, as long as they are placing orders. We don't want sales people competing with the web shop, as that would create more aggressive sales behavior that customers might not appreciate. In large accounts with high customer lifetime value, there are many extremely high-valued tasks like renewing contracts. This doesn't mean that ordering throughout the year needs to be done with human labor. Automated ordering from the customer's side can be done, when their stock levels go below a certain level. Or the customer can be trained to order from the web shop on their own, instead of relying on a sales person.

AUTOMATED AND SELF-SERVE

If a C-level customer is managed in this category, then they will not usually have an assigned account manager, but instead be fully managed by customer service on a reactive basis and they will have access to a self-service community/portal and e-commerce site for placing orders. Marketing has a great level of importance in this model, as they are responsible for keeping up the communication with the customer.

Instead of calling, meeting and sending messages manually to customers, in this model the engagement with customers happens through digital content, lots of it. The need to have a huge amount of content essential for orchestrating different customer journeys and automated messages. Without a lot of content both for sales and marketing, as well as customer support, this model will not work.

TAKING PRODUCT OR SERVICE COMPLEXITY INTO CONSIDERATION

If signing a contract or placing an order is easy, that does not mean that it's easy for a customer to commit to buying. Just because it's possible to sell something on e-commerce doesn't mean customers will buy, just because ordering is easy. The buying process up until the point when it's time to order can be quite complex. Implementing whatever the customer is buying so that it creates the needed value may be difficult to achieve. Value and risk typically go hand in hand, and risky deals create longer buying processes, because it's not just about the risk of financial losses, but the opportunity cost of making poor decisions. This is what slows buying processes down, and this must be taken into consideration when deciding what should and what should not be automated.

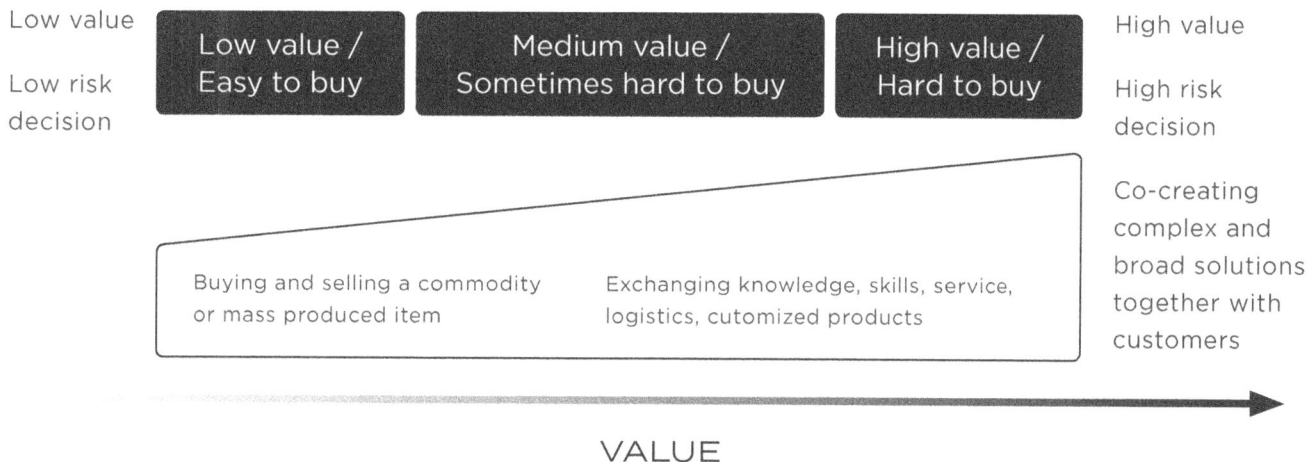

Low value / Easy to buy	Medium value / Sometimes hard to buy	High value / Hard to buy

Low value

Low risk decision

High value

High risk decision

Co-creating complex and broad solutions together with customers

Buying and selling a commodity or mass produced item

Exchanging knowledge, skills, service, logistics, cutomized products

VALUE

LOW VALUE / EASY TO BUY

For low-price commodity items, a vendor must sell large quantities of products to stay in business. Typically, if a company only has low-margin products, the amount of attention that can be given to customers that do not order large quantities must be minimized. For low-value items a mass marketing approach is ideal and only customers with high order volumes have a dedicated account manager. If the customer base is spread out, then the only option is to rely on marketing and self-serve e-commerce to make the model economically feasible. This is what the automate and self-serve approach is for.

MEDIUM VALUE / SOMETIMES HARD TO BUY

The middle is what some call "no-man's land", because sometimes it becomes hard to decide whether to rely on marketing or traditional field sales to sell. For many, the no-man's land is taken care of by inside sales, who can quite efficiently help customers decide remotely. In the United States, inside sales has become a standard way of selling because of geographical distances, while in Europe many are still used to having face-to-face meetings. In this category the products or services sold are valued between $1,000–10,000. If a sales process requires lots of human work – with meetings and travel – one deal quickly becomes unprofitable, unless the customer continuously makes orders or has signed up for a subscription service with a longer lifetime value than the original contract period.

HIGH VALUE / HARD TO BUY

This category contains solutions worth hundreds of thousands or millions, or a customer with a higher lifetime value. Here it makes sense to use people in key parts of the process, such as identifying customer needs and navigating the customers towards a good decision, as well as growing the customer. For example, some of the solutions that KONE sells can be placed in this category. In March 2018 KONE won an order for the metro line in Zhengzhou, which consisted of 64 TransitMaster™ escalators and 13 MonoSpace® elevators, and two MiniSpace™ elevators.[*]

OPTIMIZE CUSTOMER MANAGEMENT ACCORDING TO SEGMENT AND CUSTOMER VOLUME

The next graph gives an overall concept view on which customers should be given more personal attention, and which should be managed more on a self-serve basis. To keep it simple, these three customer segments are the same ones we used in Chapter 6. This model is over-simplified to make it easier to reflect on your own situation and come up with development ideas.

The point of the graph is to show roughly how much of which customer segment is managed in which way. The round circle with the customer segment represents how many of the customers in a specific segment are managed in which way.

So, for the C-segment, a small number of those customers are managed with a hybrid model, in which a person is in touch with them, but this is only roughly for 10-20% of C-segment customers.

A highly valuable customer may be handled with a personal touch in the first phases, while after converting they are managed with a fully automated process. The role of technology and human touch will vary throughout the lifecycle, and the key is to have an optimal model planned out, to guide the customers, but have the capability to serve as needed depending on the situation.

[*] www.kone.com/en/news-and-insights/releases/kone-wins-further-orders-for-zhengzhou-metro-line-in-china-2018-03-09-2.aspx

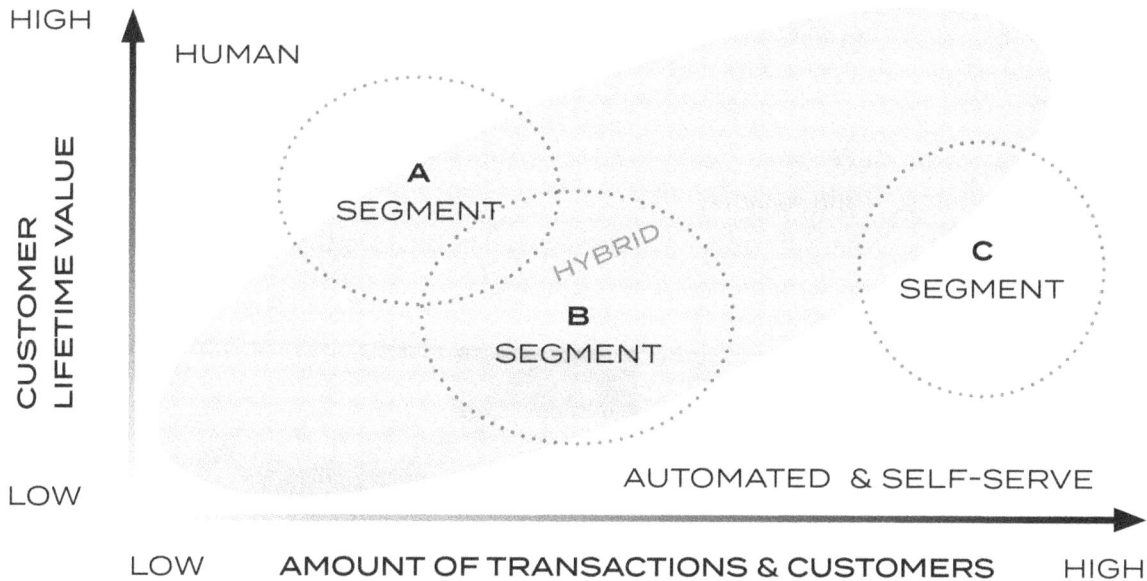

Here is a sample of what can happen in each of the customer lifecycle phases using Surf Air as an example.

SAMPLE CASE, SURF AIR (This case is not based on an interview or facts, its purpose is to demonstrate what each of the phases mean in an easy-to-understand way.)

1. Attract
A marketing executive for a large company who does a fair share of business flying (let's just call him Mike) sees an ad about Surf Air on YouTube, but doesn't click on it. The next day Mike sees a different ad on YouTube, also from Surf Air. He clicks on it and lands on Surf Air's website and impatiently scrolls down to notice the 'Unlimited flights, one monthly fee' as well as the promise of saving time and only needing to arrive at the airport 15 minutes before take-off. It sounds interesting, but he decides to come back later when not in such a rush. After this it takes weeks until he is at the airport waiting for his delayed flight, and he remembers Surf Air's promise so he pulls out his phone and goes on Surf Air's website to look for more information.

Mike also remembered that someone had talked about Surf Air at a marketing conference he attended, and this made him remember the name.

2. Connect

As Mike starts doing research on his phone at the airport, he becomes very interested and searches for answers to these questions: Where do they fly? Where is my closest location? In his mind he is already thinking about questions like: Should I try them out? What's the financial benefit to me or my company?

Mike is still a bit unsure about a few details, so he decides to call Surf Air. He gets through right away without having to wait and receives good answers to his questions immediately from a friendly customer service representative. Mike doesn't feel he is ready yet, as he needs to check about this at work, so he asks to be contacted in a couple weeks.

3. Convert

The friendly customer service representative calls back a few days later with an idea. Mike is offered to take a test flight during the call, so they book that immediately while on the phone.

As Mike arrives to take the test flight he notices how smoothly his flying could be compared to his current battle once a week. As he sits on the plane he starts to think of arguments for moving over to flying with Surf Air. He does need to convince his boss this is better, as the cost will be a bit more than right now with normal flights. Mike decides that the key argument will be time saved and calculates on average how much time he spends on a monthly level. This approach works to convince his boss, so they decide to enter into an agreement with Surf Air.

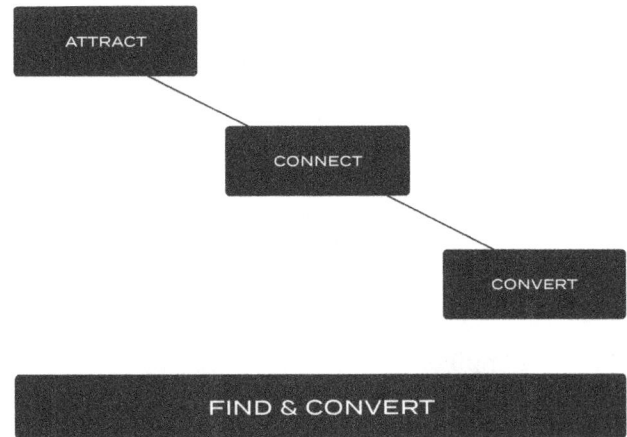

4. Onboard

Mike receives a membership package and a personal walk-through on how to use the application and how everything works so he has a 100% understanding of how to maximize the benefits of the service. The membership package and welcome process impresses Mike and he feels like he made the right choice.

5. Adopt

The first few months and year is critical for ensuring Mike attains value from the membership. He receives a membership newsletter, an occasional call from a person in the membership team, and they also meet up with Mike at the terminal a couple times during the first half-year.

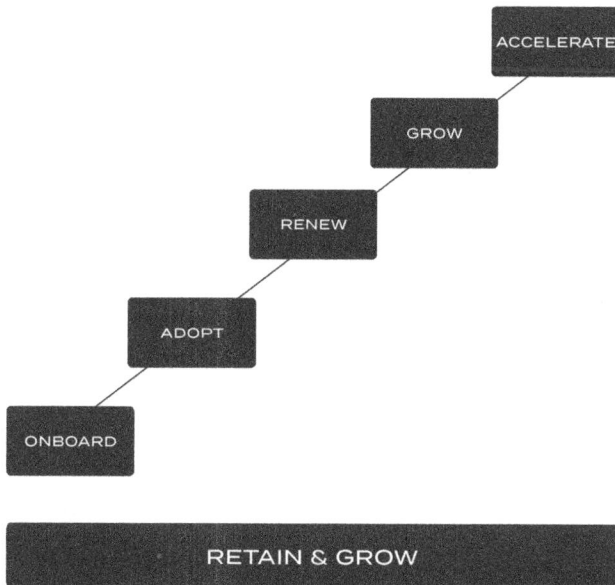

7. Grow

Since Mike is very happy, he has also recommended the service to friends and colleagues. Several other employees at Mike's place of work also sign up for a Surf Air membership.

8. Accelerate

As new airports open, Surf Air's offering becomes relevant to more offices and more employees at Mike's place of work. When there are tens or hundreds of users, Surf Air and the company start strategic joint planning to form a more valuable partnership. They plan together and ensure that the company is optimizing their travel times. They can work together to improve the membership packaging and even impact which routes and destinations will be available in the future.

As a part of their partnership with Surf Air, Mike's company's executives will be used in marketing efforts, such as customer testimonials.

ACCELERATE

GROW

RENEW

ADOPT

ONBOARD

RETAIN & GROW

6. Renew

Since Mike has been happy with Surf Air he will continue as a customer. Even if the price were to increase, there is a very high chance that he would remain a customer.

CHAPTER 8

/ BUILDING BLOCKS OF A GROWTH PLATFORM

Now that we have identified the different lifecycle stages and put some thought into segmentation it is time to start putting the building blocks of our Growth Platform into place. Although a Growth Platform is described like it is something very physical and tangible, and something that you must build, it is more of a way of thinking and developing the business than an exact formula for success. The idea is to constantly keep the customer in the center and put people, process and technology around the customer and their journey.

To improve customer experience, we need to make all the touchpoints with customers more engaging and personal. This means we need to maximize how technology can create personal experience for customers, and at the same time make sure we are maximizing the time of every person in the organization, to be able to focus on customers, and the highest value tasks. This applies no matter what kind of customer work it is, whether the person is working face-to-face, remotely, via some channel or is planning the different online journeys. You name it, we need to maximize our organization's time if we want to improve the customer experience.

Before we start building a Growth Platform for any company, it is crucial to have the customer segments identified, and agree upon how the customer management model and customer lifecycles should look. Based on this, we start the building process, and add the technology and organization. If you need more automation, then you'll stack up the technology part first. In our example in this chapter we'll place the technology part first.

PUTTING THE TECHNOLOGY INFRASTRUCTURE IN PLACE FOR YOUR PLATFORM

Up until now, many companies have used technology as tools, to help humans. Just like a hammer and shovel are tools, a CRM, for example, has been a tool for sales people. Now, technology, such as CRMs, are no longer just tools, because CRM platforms now help execute the customer journey in many automated forms and then people work on parts of the process that need a delicate, experienced and knowledgeable human touch.

Depending on what you're selling and what the optimal customer journey looks like, you need to ask the question: What is the value of having a human doing specific tasks in a particular stage of the customer's buying journey? Some businesses can build the entire attract, connect and convert stages for the whole business or for specific segments, with the help of marketing, CRM and commerce technology. This is not, however, the case for most B2B businesses. It's more of a question of which segments and which parts of customers' lifecycles can be supported by technology. It is not one or the other, it is a blend of both.

For example, it might be a reasonable decision to figure out how to automate the beginning part of the funnel until leads are converted into opportunities, after which the customer will be fully guided by the account executive.

How the different customer lifecycle stages are defined is going to guide how to build up your Growth Platform blocks and impact whether to take a people- or technology-centric approach to managing your customers throughout the lifecycle. From a concept point of view, whether your technology stack comes before your roles in the organization depends on the complexity of buying and using your products, as well as the risk or value of buying them.

Sometimes you might read or hear about "tech touch" which normally refers to customer engagement that can be automated. In the context of this book, tech also refers to the technology that supports humans in their daily work. For example, technology is supporting and guiding a sales executive when they are using a CRM to create a proposal, or managing their opportunities. Technology solutions help automate some part of customer communications which would happen through a webpage or application which is connected to a CRM, marketing automation systems and e-commerce. A fully automated customer journey could mean that a prospect sees advertising on social media, goes to the webpage, looks at a product and leaves. The next day the same product pops up in their social media feeds with the help of re-targeting advertising and finally the customer decides to buy. When the customer makes the purchase and enters their personal information, they also sign up for the company newsletter, which gives the company permission to communicate with them.

This is the start of the relationships and from this day the targeted communications will be based on purchase history and other information that is given to the company from the customer.

Technology needs to help automate as much as possible in customers' journeys, but humans need to notice when to jump in. An example of this is when someone is on a website and a bot asks what the visitor is interested in. There could be predefined questions based on the most typical types of questions that customers ask. When the bot has a conversation with the visitor, a connection has happened between the customer and the company, and this is the first 'sales engagement'. As the discussion goes forward, the bot asks why the person is visiting, so it can give the visitor more information. The bot might be able to answer or it could be that the discussion is so complex that a person is notified and jumps into the conversation. The customer service agent can help efficiently right from the start with the help of the information available from the discussion with the bot. People can think empathetically and help the customer reach a decision or solve a problem, but after the difficult things have been taken care of, technology infrastructure will help with the continuous marketing communications for the rest of the customer's lifecycle.

Just like in a factory, people now monitor and jump in if something in the process is not working or needs human assistance. Automation should be understood as a very positive thing, that is used to improve customer experience, and make smooth experiences regardless of time and place. Many tasks that require talking to humans are frustrating and time-consuming, so when done correctly it should be positive for customers and companies alike: the customer enjoys a smoother experience and companies can focus on higher-value tasks and forget about manual repetitive work. It's a win-win.

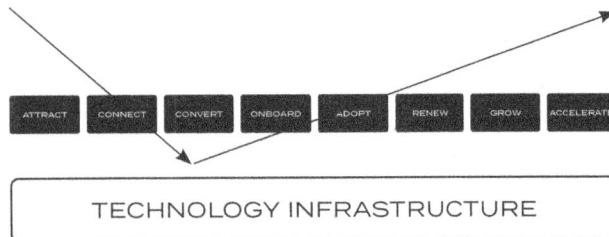

| ATTRACT | CONNECT | CONVERT | ONBOARD | ADOPT | RENEW | GROW | ACCELERATE |

TECHNOLOGY INFRASTRUCTURE

There are three reasons why the tech stack is placed first here below the lifecycle, instead of the organization and the different sales, marketing and service roles.

First, we are just so used to assigning tasks for someone to do, that often we don't think what the options for automating the task are. With artificial intelligence developing very fast, it's now time to put technology and humans on the same level, and plan what the optimal combination is, instead of always thinking of the human role first, then coming up with a way for technology to support.

The second reason for technology infrastructure to appear first in this model is for the reason that without technology the modern organization would not be capable of working together to support customers throughout the whole lifecycle and would have to operate in traditional silos. Technology is the great enabler for us to work customer-centrically, break down silos and automate certain parts of the lifecycle.

The third reason is that it's the technology infrastructure that enables certain cooperation models with customers and certain sales, marketing and service processes. While people change roles within the organization, leave the organization or new employees are hired and onboarded, the infrastructure is business-critical and slow to develop, when compared to hiring new employees. It's also more stable, in that it won't leave the company. Over 90% of Millennials (born 1977–1997) expect to only stay in a job for less than three years.[*] The more structured and process-oriented a company is, the easier it will be to onboard and develop employees, and this is increasingly important given that typical employees stay between 3–5 years. Technology helps streamline a company's way of working, and it should guide employees and make them more productive.

THE ORGANIZATION

The organization part of the platform comprises all the people in different roles in marketing, sales and customer service. These are all the people interacting with customers or responsible for planning and executing marketing or service touchpoints.

When thinking of the different stages of the customer lifecycle, which parts could not be automated and which customer segments would that include?

This is a good question because if the baseline would be that everything is automated and humans are used only for parts of the journey that need high impact, then we would more critically think about how to move customers from one stage to the next in the customer journey and what skills are needed to be able to succeed in the different roles. A skilled digital marketer will have a very different skillset than an account executive, or a customer success manager.

We should be asking ourselves: in which parts of the customer journey can humans help improve it in a way that delivers superior customer experience and differentiates us from our competitors?

What kind of roles do we need so that we can be efficient at creating customer demand, filling the funnel with leads, developing opportunities that turn into won deals, and growing our existing customers?

We will look more at the roles in Chapter 9 – Re-designing roles to support the customer journey.

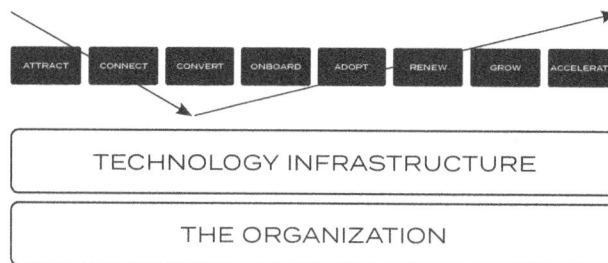

ATTRACT CONNECT CONVERT ONBOARD ADOPT RENEW GROW ACCELERATE

TECHNOLOGY INFRASTRUCTURE

THE ORGANIZATION

THE COMPLETE GROWTH PLATFORM

The capacity of a company to execute customer journeys comes from its Growth Platform. This platform combines automated processes and different marketing, sales and service roles in the organization, enabled by technology.

[*] www.forbes.com/sites/jeannemeister/2012/08/14/the-future-of-work-job-hopping-is-the-new-normal-for-millennials/#47bc13a913b8

A Growth Platform with its roles and automated processes should be able to execute different types of customer journeys and still have the flexibility when needed to be able to serve customers who have numerous ways of buying and using your products and services. Not one customer relationship or journey will ever be exactly the same!

With a platform you can connect and stay connected with the customer throughout the whole customer journey. The companies that can connect with customers and constantly engage are the winners in the age of the customer. No matter what your business model is, building a proper platform to guide your customers from one stage to the next will give you great benefits. Once you have built a platform you can bring your different types of products and services into it more easily and have greater control over all customer lifecycles. It will be possible to introduce and test new products and services more easily. Your products and services will become a part of your Growth Platform. This is what additionally enables scala-

ble and predictable growth. What you will have is a scalable organization and scalable products. The ultimate Growth Platforms have products and services completely connected to customers through the platform.

The more connected a company is to its customers through its products, systems and people, the better it can grow. This is the key point in building a Growth Platform. You can grow, due to the connectivity on multiple levels with the different customer segments.

The benefits can be compared to that of a processes-oriented manufacturing plant that can scale production as they want, combined with the finesse and human touch of an artist who makes everything by hand.

Ultimately, a Growth Platform benefits customers by creating a great customer experience, and benefits the company with predictable and scalable growth opportunities.

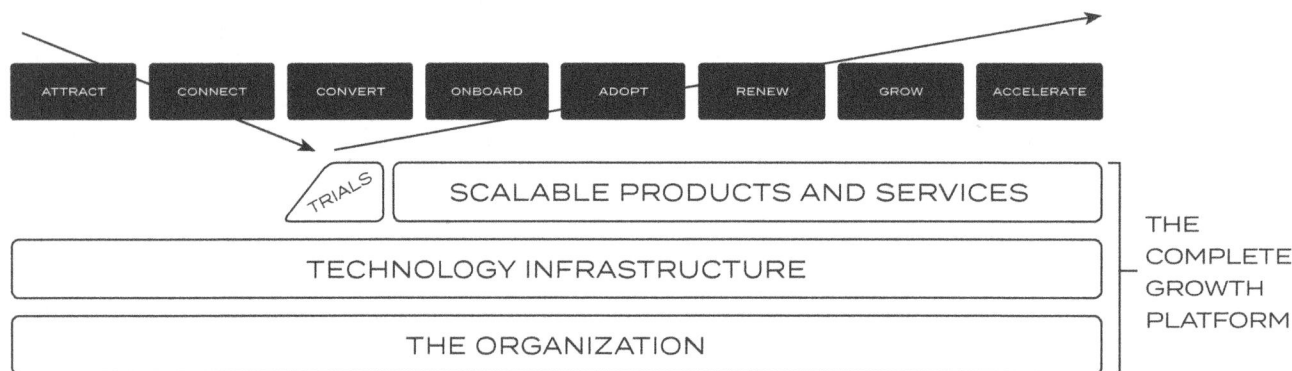

| ATTRACT | CONNECT | CONVERT | ONBOARD | ADOPT | RENEW | GROW | ACCELERATE |

TRIALS

SCALABLE PRODUCTS AND SERVICES

TECHNOLOGY INFRASTRUCTURE

THE ORGANIZATION

THE COMPLETE GROWTH PLATFORM

Whether you have continuous services or just transactional products, it makes sense in any case to build the business with platform thinking. Becoming better connected with customers through the commercial organization is the first step towards building a Growth Platform. Step two (if possible and a part of your strategy) is to be as connected as possible through the continuous products and services you provide.

Now that we have mapped the customer lifecycle stages, talked about segmenting, and identified the components of a growth platform, we are prepared to build the perfect organization suitable for managing different customers.

As stated in the beginning of this chapter, Growth Platform thinking is a new way of developing the business around the customers lifecycle, and keeping people and technology in mind continuously. People and technology are the symbiosis of modern B2B organizations. One cannot live without the other, and together, they are more than by themselves, in other words 1+1=3.

In the next part of the book we will look at building the scalable commercial organization and then walk through the different technology infrastructure components in more detail.

PART III

PUTTING THE RIGHT ROLES, PROCESSES AND TECHNOLOGY IN YOUR PLATFORM

CHAPTER 9

RE-DESIGNING ROLES TO SUPPORT THE CUSTOMER JOURNEY

Economist Adam Smith famously wrote about how an innovation around the division of labor can grow the economy. Smith used an example of a pin factory to explaining this. He claimed that ten workers produced in total 48,000 pins per day when each of the eighteen specialized tasks in the production processes were assigned to specific roles. Therefore, the average productivity would be 4,800 pins per worker per day. Without the division of labor, a worker would produce only 10–20 pins per day.[*] This is a quite powerful example of how specialization can improve efficiency.

In a traditional organization, customer-facing employees were mostly direct sales representatives who were responsible for all the customers. Sales representatives would find, sell, market, even send postcards to customers to maintain the relationship, be a customer service rep when issues came up and even fulfill orders. This meant that in earlier times sales people were only using a fraction of their time for selling as they were doing much more than just selling. Of course, there were service managers and customer service, but taking care of the customers was the responsibility of the sales person. In this model, the sales person owned the relationship and the company was dependent on the relationship that was formed between customer and salesperson, and dependent also on all the information inside the sales person's head.

In the modern organization we need to not only maximize selling time, but also maximize the impact of everything that happens along the customer journey. This calls for a major change in how organizations are set up, with new roles and responsibilities. When setting up a modern organization, the cost of sale can be radically improved. The new organization is no longer only human-intensive, but more of a blend of human and technology performing different tasks along the customer journey. Almost all companies have a wide variety of customers. Some customers need a more consultative approach, while others haven't even recognized that they have problems needing to be solved. Unless you aggressively pursue these prospects to help them out they will never buy. Then again, others know exactly what they need and they just want a smooth buying experience.

These two scenarios mentioned are radically different, so why would you have the same sales model for both?

Acquiring a new customer in a highly competitive market requires a different approach and skillset than strategic account management. The highly independent customer has put pressure on sales organizations to change, especially from a marketing perspective. Many organizations have already made big shifts in the roles and responsibilities of the commercial organization, while others have not changed enough. To build up an optimal organization with the correct roles, we must understand customer buying better. The challenge is not typically in splitting up the different parts of the customer journey into clearly different phases, but rather deciding what should be automated and what should still be done by a person to achieve an optimal buying experience for the customer. Furthermore, deciding what needs a specific role and how specific and focused that role should be is also an important decision to make.

Even the term sales role, is becoming very blurry, because a highly skilled marketing person in most industries can have a much larger positive impact on specific parts of the customer's buying process, than for example one field sales person ever could. These marketers are the growth hackers that are much talked about today. The higher volume the business, the less the traditional model makes sense. Imagine one skilled marketing person generating hundreds of leads per day, versus the traditional way that sales people would call and visit prospects when online lead generation was still basically non-existent.

Marketing, sales and service are all 'sales' roles, as they impact customer purchasing and should be managed as revenue producing roles.

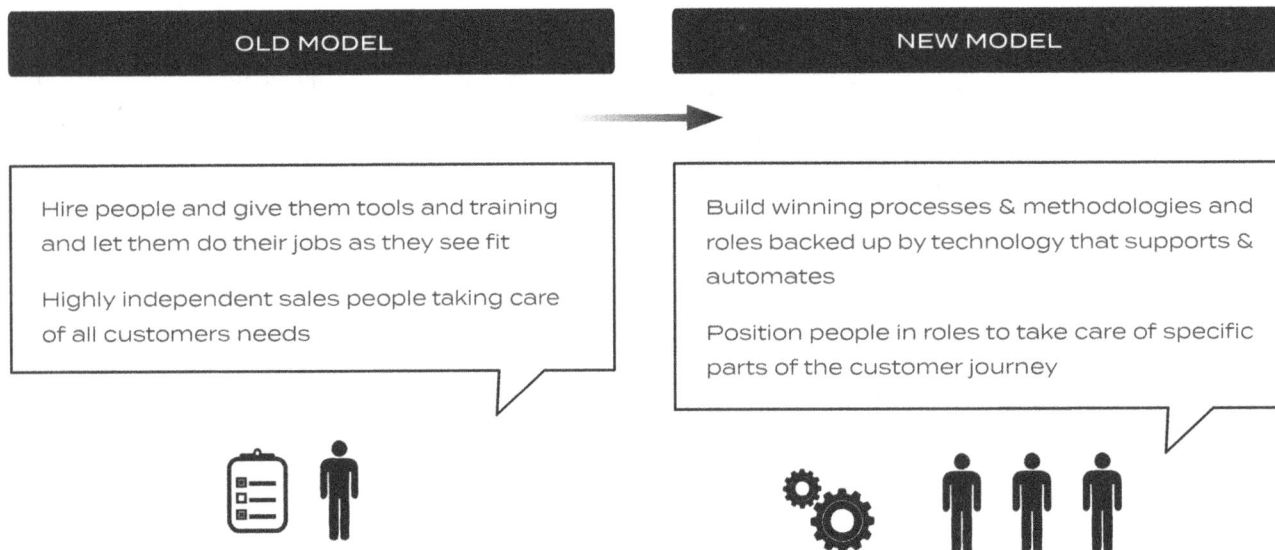

OLD MODEL

Hire people and give them tools and training and let them do their jobs as they see fit

Highly independent sales people taking care of all customers needs

NEW MODEL

Build winning processes & methodologies and roles backed up by technology that supports & automates

Position people in roles to take care of specific parts of the customer journey

SCALING GROWTH

If you want to be able to acquire and grow customers consistently and predictably, then there must be specific roles and processes in place for each stage of the customer lifecycle.

Earlier, when a company wanted to grow revenue, increasing the headcount would be a must. More sales people would be hired to take care of more territories and product lines. Sales people were back then the main point of contact for customers and all other functions were supporting sales reps. At the same time as sales people were very important, they were also a bottleneck for growth.

The old sales model didn't scale, but the Growth Platform does.

THE ERA OF SCIENCE IN SALES HAS BEGUN

As managing the customer lifecycle has become more complex and more critical, it is no longer enough to rely only on the skills of individuals. Instead, companies must rely on excellent processes that are executed by specialists in different parts of the customer lifecycle. With processes companies can multiply success, and divide people's responsibilities to increase the efficiency of every individual.

This is quite like what happened in the era of mass production. Instead of having all people in the factory assembling products independently, they began focusing on one task that they became experts at. Each part of the manufacturing process was split into many small processes. Without processes to rely on and develop, it is hard to scale. The goal should be to run sales as a science, not an art.

"When you get the right ratio down with the channels and messaging, you basically have a money printing machine"

-Niklas Sluijter, CMO

The goal is to have a scalable organization that is set up and organized in such a way that once you get the formula right, you have a money printing platform in place.

IMAGINING THE CUSTOMER JOURNEY AS A PRODUCTION LINE

Modernizing the commercial organization is essentially about reordering how sales, marketing and customer service work together. The reordering is like how Henry Ford reordered Ford Motor Company's assembly line. This same shift of mass production is our goal when building a Growth Platform: splitting up the old organization into specific tasks and roles, supported by technology, to make customer engagement highly scalable.

In the modern production era Toyota Production Systems became famous for its production processes and methods, which are similar to the types of processes and methods that are being brought into sales and marketing now. Toyota Production Systems has concepts like Kaizen, Muda, Pokayoke, Kanban.* Kaizen, for example, means a system of continuous improvement in which instances of Muda (waste) are eliminated one-by-one at minimal cost. Sounds a lot like growth hacking, with the goal of maximizing resources and continuously improving marketing results based on data.

This same type of continuous process improvement or Kaizen needs to be implemented in sales, marketing and service. The amount of transparency we now have in sales, marketing and service will make it possible to make similar improvements, since the customer lifecycle can be broken down into a series of processes that can be improved incrementally all at the same time. These are a few benefits and reasons why fast-growing modern companies rely more on their winning processes, backed up by people that are trained to succeed in specific parts of the sales process.

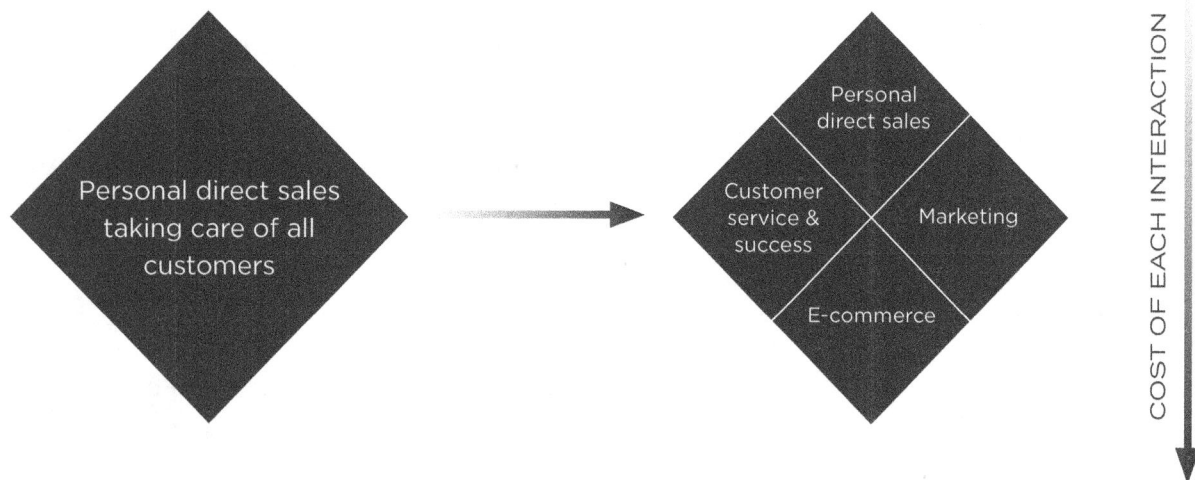

* en.wikipedia.org/wiki/Toyota_Production_System

INTERVIEW: JAAKKO PAALANEN, CHIEF SALES OFFICER AT LEADFEEDER

ABOUT LEADFEEDER

Leadfeeder is a software company that helps companies identify website visitors. For more information visit www.leadfeeder.com

WHAT IS THE RELATIONSHIP BETWEEN SALES AND MARKETING AT LEADFEEDER?

Our marketing aligns with what we call the 'sales machine'. In our line of business, if marketing doesn't work then sales does not work either. They are fully dependent on each other and we have a very transparent funnel that is shared across sales, marketing and customer success so that everybody can understand the different parts of the funnel.

HOW HAVE YOU BUILT YOUR CUSTOMER JOURNEY AT LEADFEEDER?

First, we drive traffic to our website from different sources such as social media, Google organic search, paid search, PR and newsletters. Then we convert these visitors into trial users and this is where the sign-up process happens. We have a 14-day free trial for companies to fully try out our product. During that period, we market the full premium features so that users fully understand our capabilities. We use intelligence during the onboarding phase so we can tell exactly which trial users need more hand-holding and support, while others are left in a more automated customer management model.

During the trial we encourage users to share information about us in social media and in return they get an extended trial or cashback. This has been a good way to get people to spread the word about us already in the trial period. Technically it's just a unique link, through which a new user must sign up to get the trial extension or cashback. At the end of the trial we let the users know what they are losing out on if they do not move over to a premium account and choose to only use the free version.

HOW IMPORTANT IS ONBOARDING?

"Onboarding is everything."

We use Intercom to orchestrate and automate the whole onboarding process. We can welcome the user early on and teach them how to use our tool with automated messages. Based on what they are doing with our product, we can trigger different types of messages. For example, if we see that a customer is not using some type of feature that they could be benefiting from, we send them an automated reminder that tells them about how the features could be helping them. When they try it out, we send them a congratulations message to let them know they did a good job.

See more about this in Chapter 10 -
Marketing and customer success become crucial

IS THERE A DIFFERENT PROCESS FOR DIFFERENT TYPES OF CUSTOMERS?

Yes. For SMBs we rely on our automated process, but for enterprises we proactively get in touch with them to offer them personal help. So far, we have had two different automated paths, but now there is a third also. We call them high-touch, mid-touch, no-touch (from a human perspective).

See more about this in Chapter 6 –
Customer segmentation

TO DEVELOP YOUR SALES, HAVE YOU DONE CUSTOMER JOURNEY MAPPING?

Our data tells us everything about the customer journey and our main tool has been our joint funnel. We know from which sources the most valuable customers come and we know what all customers are doing during the trials. Recently we shifted over from a 30-day trial to a 14-day trial because we noticed that the activities cus-

tomers need to complete to make a decision were actually done in just two weeks' time, so it made sense to make the trial period shorter and quickly convert satisfied trial users.

HOW HAVE YOU ORGANIZED YOUR ROLES AND MANAGEMENT?

We have a customer success and product lead, then me from the sales side and our marketing lead and we all get together monthly for our funnel conversion meeting. Together we've mapped the whole process from marketing all the way to customer success. In the marketing team we have a paid marketing expert, who optimizes our analytics usage, paid advertisement and Google and social media ads. We have a couple of content people who are responsible for our messaging and they were very important from early on. Our marketing lead is very hands-on involved in the day-to-day marketing development.

WHAT ARE THE ROLES IN YOUR SALES TEAM?

It has been possible to build this business model without having sales guys chasing customers. Our sales guys are in business development roles. They are, for example, doing 30-minute trainings with trial customers who request training. These are very important to us, because when we offer these trainings we have a 50% conversion rate.

They are also in charge of our weekly webinar. This is for our no-touch customers. For mid-touch we offer 30-minute trainings. With enterprise customers we work very proactively, so from the moment they sign up for a trial we try to be in touch with them within five minutes.

In our sales machine, we try to keep the customers in the training funnel and enterprise separate to give enough focus. For trial users who have not logged any activity in three days, we proactively get in touch with them to make sure the probability of converting is as high as possible.

WHAT ARE EACH OF YOUR ROLES?

The job of marketing is to create new trial sign-ups and that is the main KPI. Creating brand awareness and word-of-mouth is also good, but the main goal of marketing is to drive traffic to our website and convert them into trial users. I think a mistake that many companies make is that they try to get as many sign-ups as possible. For us it is the quality of the conversion that allows us to operate so efficiently on the sales side. Qualified sign-ups are essential for us. If they have a certain type of account, then it's not counted in sales conversions. We have lots of transparency in what is qualified and what is not.

If marketing cannot feed qualified leads, then our sales machine doesn't work. Sales helps marketing because our sales team is responsible for our partner companies. Our sales people are responsible for getting our partner companies to create content about us, so the sales team also helps to create content which means we can generate more traffic and sign-ups.

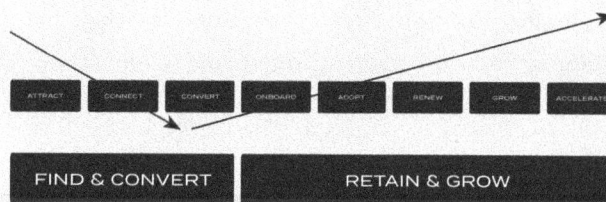

ATTRACT CONNECT CONVERT ONBOARD ADOPT RENEW GROW ACCELERATE

FIND & CONVERT   RETAIN & GROW

WHAT ARE YOUR SUGGESTIONS FOR A LEADER IN A TRADITIONAL SALES ORGANIZATION IF THEY WANT TO BUILD A MODERN SALES MACHINE?

Firstly, they should build a closer relationship between sales and marketing. Marketing should have at least some responsibility for generating revenue. That would put pressure on marketing to produce higher-quality leads for example. When it comes to sales people, they should understand marketing better and do marketing activities themselves by using their social profiles and learning about the customers. It is getting harder and harder every day to reach someone via phone. I'm not saying that cold calling is dead, but it is getting much tougher.

See more about this in Chapter 10 – Marketing and customer success become crucial

ROLES IN THE MODERN ORGANIZATION

In a modern organization there can be many different people who are responsible for parts of the sales process that a sales representative was previously responsible for. This has led to new roles being created such as inbound marketing specialist, market development representative, account-based marketing manager, growth hacker, SDR (sales development representative), BDR (business development representative), pre-sales engineer, inside sales executive, account executive, key account executive, strategic account manager, global account manager, customer success manager, and customer service agent.

OLD

CUSTOMER AND PROSPECTS

Sales reps

Marketing, service, back-office
and other functions

NEW

CUSTOMER AND PROSPECTS

Marketing, sales, service and customer success

SUPPORTED MAINLY BY
AUTOMATED TECHNOLOGY

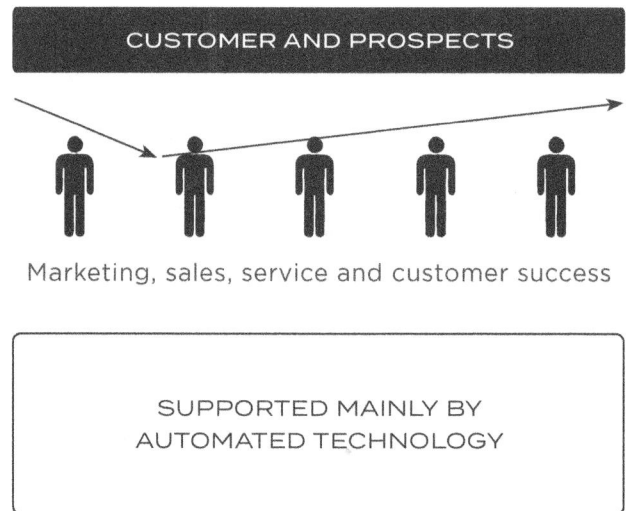

Depending on your company size and the complexity of what you sell you will have to figure out the most efficient way to divide responsibilities. In small startups, it may be a good idea if one person or a few people take care of the whole broad range of tasks related to marketing, sales and service. When the company starts to scale one person at a time, there will be a lot of opportunities to split up responsibilities and then the roles laid out here in this part will make more sense. In a small company, you could for example have one person doing marketing, while in a larger organization a large team of different individuals should be focusing on specific marketing tasks, such as lead qualification.

Here is a list with examples of many different roles that are found within a modern organization.

Role	Examples of work tasks	Objectives
Inbound marketing specialist	Creating search engine and social media friendly content that generates inbound traffic and leads. Managing campaigns and marketing automation	Generate leads for the sales team
Account based marketer	Planning and executing marketing campaigns to support pipeline and lead generation from specific accounts	Creating demand in new (typically larger) accounts
Inside sales	Selling remotely to specific customer segments Cold-calling, emailing, holding online meetings and reaching prospects remotely	Reach target revenue quota from new accounts and/or existing accounts
Business development representative (aka BDR)	Qualifying and working on accounts up to a specific point where it makes sense to bring in the account executive	Qualifying a specific amount of business that converts to opportunities for account executives.
Pre-sales engineer	Supporting account executives in their sales efforts and bringing a technical level of expertise that is required to also discuss with the technical people on the customers side.	Help with discovery and scoping the correct solutions for customers
Account executive	Depending on the industry and deal size, account executives can be broadly responsible both for prospecting new accounts, creating demand and also capturing demand, so getting customers to sign the contracts. This is a very versatile role, but in some organizations account executives only focus on closing deals that marketing has generated and nurtured until they are at a certain stage	Reach target revenue quota from new accounts and/or existing accounts
Customer success manager	Onboarding customers to ensure that products are adopted immediately in the beginning of taking the products or services in use. Provide customers reactive and proactive help with using products through the whole lifecycle to maximize the value they are getting.	Onboarding Decreasing customer churn and increasing customer satisfaction of the products and services in use by the customer Up-selling and cross-selling (in some companies)

Role	Examples of work tasks	Objectives
Customer service agent	Handling and solving inbound calls and emails about issues, complaints, questions. Answering comments and complaints in social media	Solve problems & keep customers happy Upselling and cross-selling (in some companies)
Happy bot	Doing simple manual work 24/7 on websites like answering questions and directing customers to the right content on the website. The bot can also help with scheduling meetings and handing over qualified prospects to sales while the prospect is on your website.	Enable fast and dependable service Minimize the need for human interaction in simply and manual tasks Lead qualification and hand-over

DIFFERENT SKILLSETS IN DIFFERENT PARTS OF THE CUSTOMERS LIFECYCLE

The old model was to have sales training seminars for sales people, and then throw them out to see if they would succeed. Sales training used to be very broad, because the responsibility of sales was very broad. Five days of training could be spent learning about everything from pricing to cold calling. Now role-specific processes and training give a higher chance that individuals and organizations will succeed. Customer acquisition or customer retention is so difficult, that it demands dedicated roles with dedicated KPIs that are constantly monitored and improved.

In the next graph you see depicted a simple and straightforward way of organizing the roles around the phases of the customer lifecycle. It shows how the responsibilities of traditional sales organizations have been split into different types of roles with more specific responsibilities.

The simpler the product and its usage, the easier it is to have an organizational setup like this. As mentioned earlier, the first phases of attracting, connecting and converting are quite straightforward to divide by different responsibilities and stages, like a production line. Once the relationship officially starts, there can be many different types of cooperation models among marketing, sales and customer success depending on the product or service you sell and the segments you serve.

```
ATTRACT
    CONNECT
        CONVERT
                    ONBOARD
                        ADOPT
                            RENEW
                                GROW
                                    ACCELERATE
```

TECHNOLOGY INFRASTRUCTURE

| Marketing | Sales | Customer success | Customer success (CS) or CS together with sales and marketing |

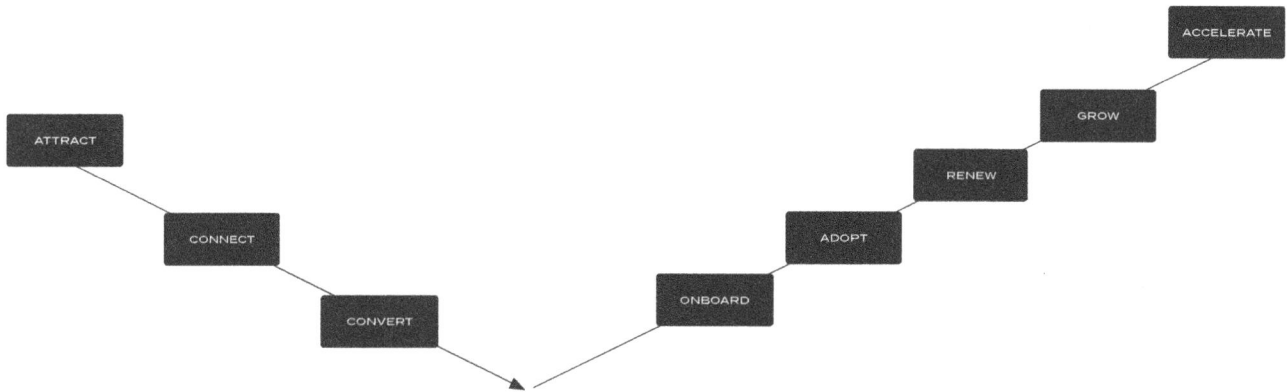

PRODUCTION LINE WITH HANDOVERS

TEAM WORK ON STRATEGIC ACCOUNTS & CLEAR OWNERSHIP OF SPECIFIC ACTIVITIES

ACQUIRING NEW CUSTOMERS

DIVIDING THE RESPONSIBILITIES BETWEEN SALES AND MARKETING

Looking at the different tasks and activities – from attracting, to connecting, to converting – a typical setup for a B2B company could have three different types of roles to manage this. Marketing helps create demand in the market and attracts customers to the company. As visitors become leads, business development can qualify and evaluate whether the prospect is a good fit and whether they should be moved over to an account executive to convert. This is a very typical model in software sales, whereas in other industries there may not be a business development representative between marketing and account executive. In general, it becomes a question of the volume of leads and how much business development and growth a company is looking to achieve. Any company that wants to grow, or is looking to maximize the time that their account executives spend on high-value tasks should have a layer between marketing and the account executives. For higher-value complex solutions, it can make sense to not have a layer between marketing and sales. This is for situations where there is only a limited number of accounts that can be worked on, and resources are very scarce. For example, the annual goal could be to acquire three major accounts. These higher-value opportunities can be pursued independently by the account executive. With lower-ticket items and services that can be purchased online there is not usually a reason to have a business development rep in between marketing and field sales.

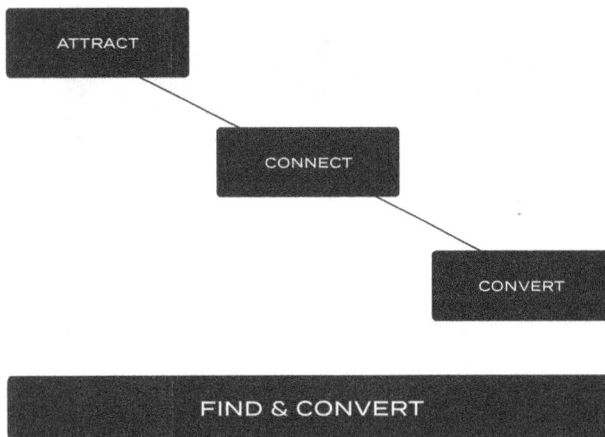

SALES PROFESSIONALS' WORK HAS BECOME MORE FOCUSED

Many have proclaimed that the sales profession is dying, but at the same time the world is becoming complex and customers need help understanding new solutions and possibilities. So, who is going to help them? Consultative sales professionals. Forrester Research published their 'Death of a (B2B) Salesman report' , which also makes this case. According to Forrester, the need for consultative sales professionals will increase by 10%, while the other types of sales professionals will decrease. These are 'order takers', 'navigators', 'explainers'. Overall from 2012 to 2020, Forrester predicted that the number of sales professionals in the US will drop from 4.5 million to 3.5 million. So, from the perspective of the whole funnel, the area of responsibility of sales executives is decreasing, because sales executives are focusing on the most important and valuable work, while marketing, service and e-commerce are doing what the order takers, navigators and explainers have been doing in many companies.

In the next graph there are three different types of situations with different responsibilities between marketing and sales.

* go.forrester.com/what-it-means/ep12-death-b2b-salesman/

VALUE & COST OF EACH INTERACTION

STAGE

ATTRACT	CONNECT	CONVERT

Low complexity

Advertising		
Content marketing		
PR		
SEO & SEM	Website visitors	Re-targeting, E-mail

MARKETING

E-COMMERCE

Mid complexity

Advertising					
Content marketing					
PR		Account based	Qualify leads		Diagnose,
Events	Inbound marketing	marketing	Contact potential	Hand over to	propose and
SEO & SEM	Website visitors	Re-targeting ads	customers	account executive	close

MARKETING | BUSINESS DEVELOPMENT REP | ACCOUNT EXECUTIVE

High complexity

Account based	High level contact			
marketing planned	approach with highly	Discovery meetings &		Negotiate
together with	valuable industry	building a mutual plan	Build proposal	
sales	specific insight	with champion		Close

MARKETING | ACCOUNT EXECUTIVE

INTERVIEW: NIKLAS SLUIJTER, CHIEF MARKETING OFFICER AT SMARP

ABOUT SMARP

Smarp is a SaaS company offering a platform that drives employee engagement and advocacy. They have customers such as KPMG, DELL EMC and Unilever.

WHAT PART OF THE CUSTOMER LIFECYCLE DOES YOUR MARKETING TEAM FOCUS ON?

We're involved throughout the entire funnel, but our main goal is to drive revenue from new business. So naturally the focus is at the beginning of the lifecycle, where we attract, educate and inspire new visitors to consider working with Smarp. After that we work together closely with our Sales and Customer Success departments to make sure our prospects have a uniform experience, and we can maximize the value.

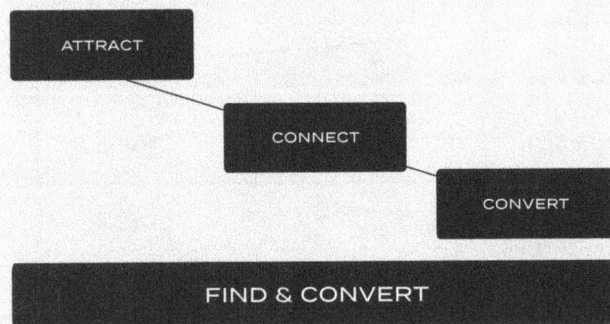

ATTRACT

CONNECT

CONVERT

FIND & CONVERT

HOW DO YOU THINK MARKETING HAS CHANGED OVER THE YEARS?

When you think about it, we're used to seeing advertisements in newspapers and magazines, with a call-to-action. Essentially, the fundamentals are the same, but technology has made it so much easier to execute complex marketing strategies in very short timespans.

In return, due to the on-demand and instant nature of the internet, people expect to get value much faster than before. To be able to keep up with that demand, companies are looking to include more self-service features and Artificial Intelligence into their products and websites.

And then of course there's the wide range of new media available, made easily accessible by technology. Literally anyone can create video advertisements, run them on several networks, and see the results right away.

IF YOU ONLY HAD TO RELY ON IN-BOUND MARKETING, WOULD YOU BE ABLE TO ACHIEVE YOUR GOAL OF DOUBLING REVENUE?

To answer this question, we need to look at how easy it is to understand the product. If your product is simple enough to understand in terms of its value, its use and how to purchase it all by yourself, then you should be good to go with a full inbound approach.

"In this inbound model when you get the right ratio down with the channels and messaging, you basically have a money printing machine."

But when the offering becomes more complex and you have more people involved in making decisions, then you most likely need a sales professional to help navigate the customer through part of the process.

HOW HAVE YOU SEGMENTED YOUR CUSTOMERS AND DO YOU HAVE DEFINED BUYER ROLES?

We do have 'the usual' split by number of employees. SMB and enterprise is split separately. SMB is for companies with 200–2000 employees and enterprise is 2000 employees and above. Anything below 200 employees falls into our self-service segment.

In marketing, we segment by departments and seniority level, and in sales we augment these with their buyer role. We always define the internal champions and supporters, as well as those who sign off on a buying decision. This ensures we have got all bases covered and are integrated into every single part of the internal buying process.

See more about this in Chapter 6 –
Customer segmentation

DO YOU HAVE JOINT KPIS WITH SALES?

At the end of the day it comes down to how much money we are spending and how much business we are getting with that money, so how much sales can close on what we bring them. This keeps our marketing team sharp and willing to learn more so we can constantly keep improving. This means that we are not just interested in the marketing part of the funnel, but we are just as interested – if not almost more interested – in the sales part, because increasing sales is what everyone is striving to achieve.

"We are not focused on leads, we are focused on generating revenue."

WHAT IS THE FORUM FOR DEVELOPING YOUR JOINT FUNNEL WITH SALES?

Together with our heads of sales and customer success we go deep into our pipeline situation every Monday. We go through what we are focusing on and what we are tweaking. This is an essential meeting, because we make decisions together that impact each other's actions. For example, at one point the sales team was fully busy with all the current leads they had, so we decided they should get more time to focus on them and we decreased the number of leads for a little while to allow them to fully focus on closing the business they had. The results were great. This discussion forum allows us to quickly make decisions that ensure we are not wasting any budget.

See more about this in Chapter 10 – Marketing and customer success become crucial

DO BIG COMPANIES HAVE AN ADVANTAGE OF SCALE BECAUSE IT'S EASIER FOR THEM TO USE TECHNOLOGY?

I think it is a misconception that only enterprises have the capabilities to create complex software stacks with interconnected systems. I can understand that since integrations have traditionally always been custom made, they have been difficult to deal with, but now we have modern cloud-based integration tools like Zapier, Cloudpipes, IFTTT and Integromat, which are really changing the game. They enable anyone to take whatever data their platforms can generate and use it however they want. It's really the large organizations that have the most difficulties in adopting or changing technologies, as they have made investments in infrastructure and systems that are highly dependent on each other. Making any changes would have significant impact on their resources and processes.

See more about this in Chapter 11 – Technology components of your Growth Platform

WHAT SHOULD MARKETERS BE EXCITED ABOUT?

Just data! The amount of data and a huge chain of numbers that affect each other is now available to be collected and analyzed. The chain might be multidimensional and all the numbers are connected. Tangible metrics are great, but now we can start interpreting and analyzing so much data that it allows us to make better decisions all the time.

Marketing is becoming more like engineering, and that should be exciting. Sales is becoming more digital and AI is coming into a more mature phase and everything companies now do is either directly or indirectly connected to marketing. It's pretty exciting now since AI and conversation bots are capable of augmenting what humans have done before. These things make marketing's role so much more holistic than ever before.

SHOULD MARKETING BE INVOLVED IN GROWING CURRENT CUSTOMERS?

I think marketing should definitely work with the data you have on current customers and think of how this data can help increase purchasing by bundling products and marketing differently to current customers. We currently happen to focus most of our efforts at Smarp on acquiring new customers, but an organization in a more stable growth phase should create content and campaigns that will increase up-selling, cross-selling and retention.

WHAT ARE YOUR KEY PIECES OF ADVICE FOR MARKETERS TO DRIVE GROWTH FOR THEIR COMPANIES?

Keep the learning curve steep; there are new technologies and opportunities arising at an increasing rate. You must keep learning and challenging the decisions you are making.

Get the data; collect data on everything and use what you can to constantly improve your results. I know GDPR hasn't made this easier, but it will skyrocket your data quality.

Be fearless; don't be afraid of trying new things and trying them often.

Pace and trust yourself; don't always trust the gurus and what everyone else is preaching. Take the time and learn what you need to learn to make informed decisions and think for yourself. Don't rely on vendors to tell you what is best for you.

GROWING CURRENT CUSTOMERS

MOVING FROM CUSTOMER ACQUISITION TO CUSTOMER MANAGEMENT

It is still quite simple to model the customer acquisition funnel and split up the responsibilities, but having clear responsibilities and roles and a picture of the funnel of existing customers is not as simple and straightforward as the customer acquisition funnel.

Depending on the business you are in, you need to balance the mix of customer and segment ownership and responsibilities between sales, marketing, customer service and customer success. Depending on your line of business, what you sell and how you have segmented your customers, the three will be mixed accordingly, but who owns existing customers?

If there are only small up-selling opportunities after the initial deal, then the customer success team should be taking care of those customers while sales focuses on acquiring new customers.

In the land-and-expand strategy, where there is also potential for large deals after acquiring a customer, there will be a great deal of consultative selling. Although there is a high level of consultative selling, this does not mean that marketing, and service/customer success wouldn't be working closely with sales. Actually, quite the opposite.

Typically, sales will own the relationship with the customer, while marketing helps fill the funnel and keeps customers in the loop, but this is not the best setup in all cases. Here are three options for different types of ways to manage the relationship after conversion.

THE THREE POTENTIAL OWNERS OF THE CUSTOMER AFTER ACQUISITION

#1 Marketing

Marketing owns the relationship when the whole path from becoming a customer to growing can be owned by marketing fully, and supported by customer service. This is typically the case in lower-ticket items, that can be purchased very independently from an e-commerce store.

#2 Customer success

After the sales executive has done their job converting the customer, customer success will own and take responsibility for the customer. They will not only ensure the customer adopts and benefits from the solution, but they will also try to cross-sell and up-sell. If there was a sales person involved in earlier phases of the sales process, they will not need to be involved after customer success steps in and a proper handover is done.

#3 Account executive (AE)

If the account executive owns the relationship, then customer success will support the account executive and they can have a very large role, but the ultimate responsibility lies with the account executive. The AE is also supported by pre-sales engineers, marketing, customer service and back-office.

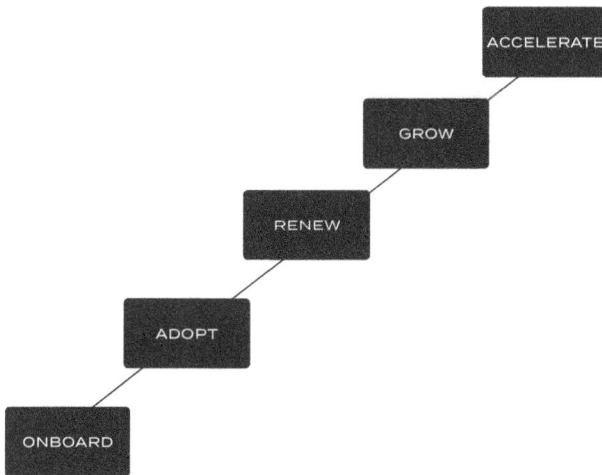

LEADING AND MANAGING THE MODERN ORGANIZATION

Leading an organization that has roles taking care of different parts of the customer's journey – all selling in one way or another – requires holistic management with the help of more specific KPIs than before. All customer-facing organizations should be understood as revenue producing, not only salespeople, and this is a big shift. There are three departments that can be firmly linked to revenue that need to be led quite differently.

These three departments fill the funnel, convert, and grow customers. In most businesses it makes sense to have someone overlooking the whole commercial operation from lead to strategic customer, while also having different leaders for filling the funnel, converting and growing customers.

A shift from the traditional sales role being at the center of the organization is coming to an end, and every customer interaction is now an opportunity to sell more. Due to the need for more holistic leadership, there are new leadership roles now in many organizations, such as chief customer officer, chief sales officer or chief revenue officer.

Without breaking down the walls between your different functions and leading them as one revenue unit, your Growth Platform will get clogged up and parts won't work. That will manifest itself in unsatisfied customers, and thus the rise of the chief revenue officer is a good development. Revenue should be managed more holistically as customers should not belong to a department, but rather have a consistent and unified journey.

KPIS FOR LEADING

By breaking down the customer lifecycle into the two main categories: acquisition and growth, it's easier to set clear KPIs for each department and clear KPIs for each role within the departments.

When there are many different departments or teams, they need to be aligned in the KPIs so that there is a forward-looking chain that focuses on joint goals. Too often marketing has, for example, goals of certain activities, but they do not measure the impact of the activities all the way to revenue being produced. Everyone needs to be fully aligned with KPIs and these need to be aligned with the overall commercial goals of the business.

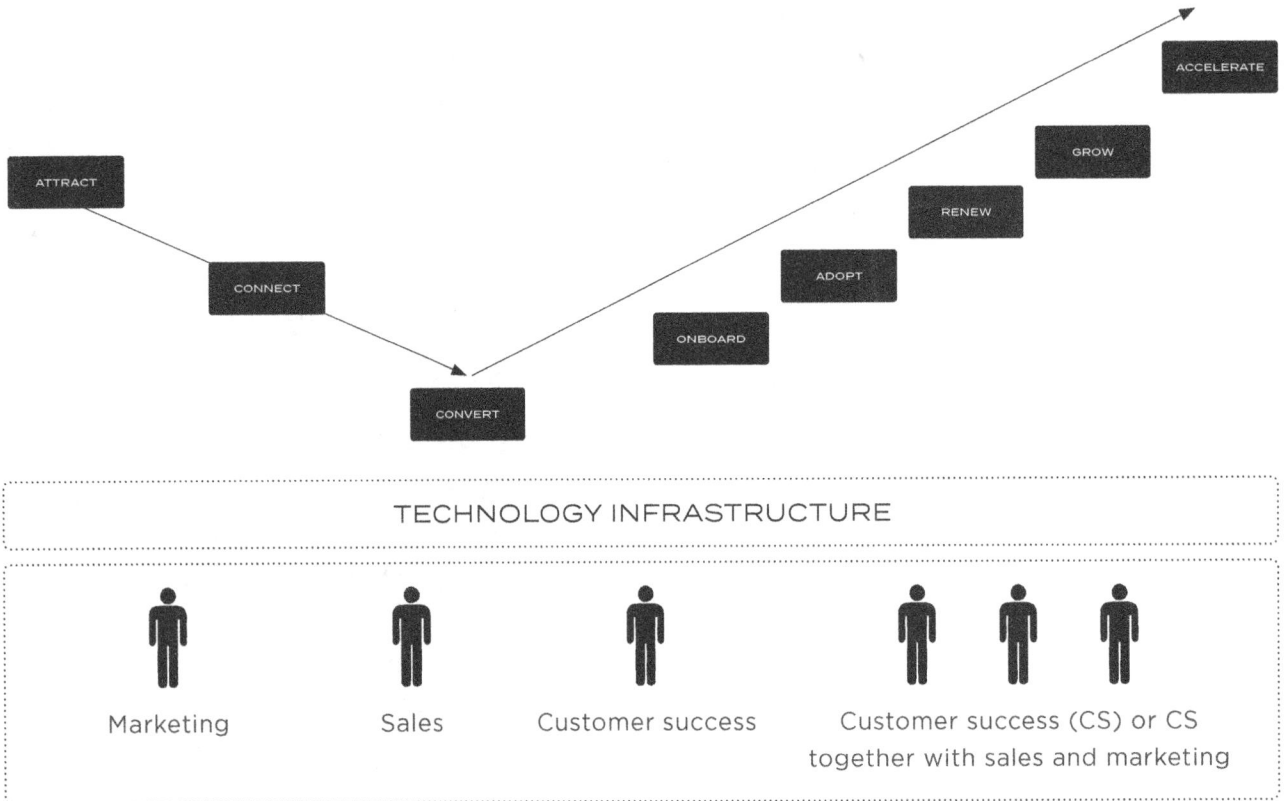

ATTRACT

CONNECT

CONVERT

ONBOARD

ADOPT

RENEW

GROW

ACCELERATE

TECHNOLOGY INFRASTRUCTURE

Marketing

Sales

Customer success

Customer success (CS) or CS together with sales and marketing

CHAPTER 10

/ MARKETING AND CUSTOMER SUCCESS BECOME CRUCIAL

We have dedicated this chapter to both marketing and customer success because these are the two major areas that require extra focus and development work in many B2B companies.

Customer behavior has changed so fast that many companies have not been able to adjust the role and tasks of marketing and consider how sales and marketing should cooperate. Customers are highly independent, so it makes sense most often to give more responsibility to marketing to create content and manage the top of the funnel, while sales executives focus on less scalable work like diagnosing what a specific customer needs and doing what needs to be done to win a contract. The skillsets needed for creating leads and solution selling are very different, so it makes sense to split up the responsibilities.

As customers have become more empowered, solutions have also become more complex and customers have more options than ever. This is why customer success has become crucial. An organization must ensure customers are gaining the value from their solutions right from the start. In this chapter we'll hear more thoughts about this from a customer success pioneer, Salesforce, and what their VP and Regional Leader of Cus-tomer Success Group EMEA North says about the fundamentals of customer success.

If you are interested in reading more about customer success than what's on offer in this book, take a look at the book: Customer Success: How Innovative Companies Are Reducing Churn and Growing Recurring Revenue, by Nick Mehta, Dan Steinman and Lincoln Murphy.

CUSTOMER LIFECYCLE STAGES

Sales executives only focus here

ATTRACT · CONNECT · CONVERT · ONBOARD · ADOPT · RENEW · GROW · ACCELERATE

FIND & CONVERT   RETAIN & GROW

MARKETING

INCREASE THE RESPONSIBILITY OF MARKETING

Compared with the other sections in this part of the book we will be covering the topic of marketing the most since this is an area where many B2B companies are struggling the most. This is because the customer age demands a more marketing-driven approach to selling. This doesn't, however, mean a more passive approach. This is where many understand incorrectly. The means of using content, and creating marketing permission doesn't need to be passive.

Earlier marketing was really just about getting attention and creating interest at the top of the funnel. Sales people would be out in the field selling and taking orders. These days marketing should be a part of every stage of the funnel, not just at the top, but in the middle and even at the end. With the capabilities that digital technologies provide, it should not only be an opportunity, but a necessity to increase the transparency of marketing results and the accountability of marketing.

FORGET MASS MARKETING AND EMBRACE PERSONALIZED MARKETING

From a marketing communications perspective, the mass production and mass marketing era was all about creating main messages about a product and making sure enough people heard about the product by getting good coverage with traditional media. There was not an abundance of products and options for consumers so there was no real compelling need to connect on a personal level. Competition was not so tough, so mass marketing was enough. Now in the digital world with CRM and marketing automation, the opportunity to target, connect and convert customers are countless and hyper effective. A company can target its competitors' customers as easily as setting up keyword advertising in Google or going after competitors' customers via social channels with great targeting capabilities.

In many industries there have been multiple layers or channels between the producer of the product or service and the end customer. For example, a manufacturer would traditionally sell their equipment to dealers or sometimes there would also be someone between them as well, but now equipment manufacturers are creating applications and services to connect directly with the end customers.

MARKETING SHOULD NOT ONLY SUPPORT, BUT BE RESPONSIBLE FOR DRIVING REVENUE

Marketing should generate revenue in three ways:

1. Indirectly, by generating leads, as well as cross-sell and up-sell opportunities that turn into revenue

2. Generating sales directly via e-commerce or portals.

3. Nurture opportunities that develop into won opportunities.

The simpler the product or service is, the more responsibility marketing should have when looking at the funnel. Where complex deal navigation is needed, then the role of marketing will be smaller, and have an indirect impact. In this case marketing could have more of an account-based approach, which would mean that marketing together with sales would decide on specific accounts that needed to be penetrated. Marketing can have a huge impact on accelerating new strategic accounts when done correctly.

High complexity

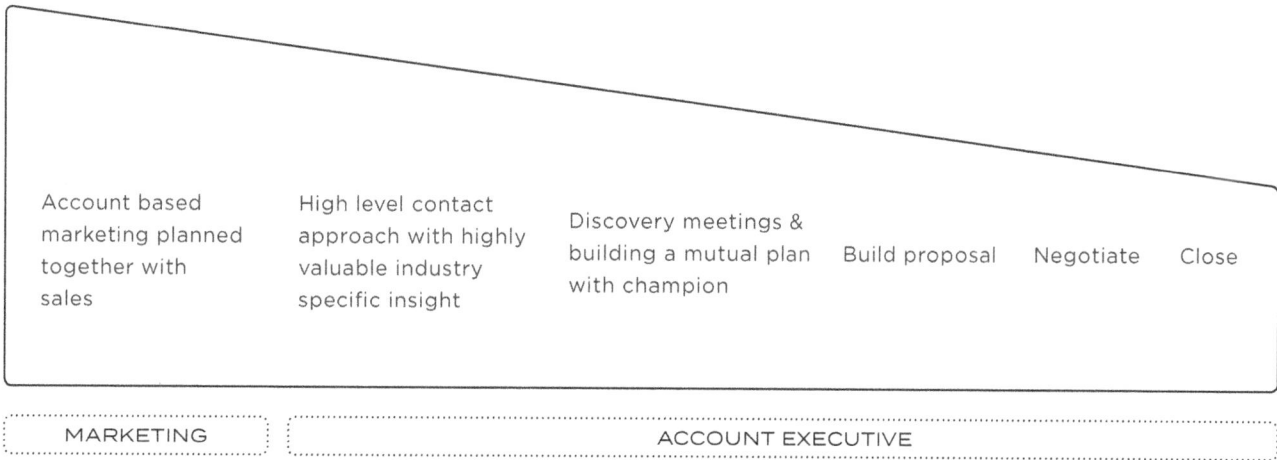

Account based marketing planned together with sales

High level contact approach with highly valuable industry specific insight

Discovery meetings & building a mutual plan with champion

Build proposal

Negotiate

Close

MARKETING

ACCOUNT EXECUTIVE

KILL THE SILOS AND HAVE A JOINT FUNNEL WITH SALES

In the next picture you see one funnel. Very often the concepts of funnel and pipeline get mixed up, so this picture helps clear things up. The key here is that marketing and sales should together plan how the business goals will be reached and who is responsible for what in the funnel and pipeline and how it will be measured.

The funnel helps with planning, it may be contradictory to the lifecycle model, but especially for new customer acquisition it is a concept that helps.

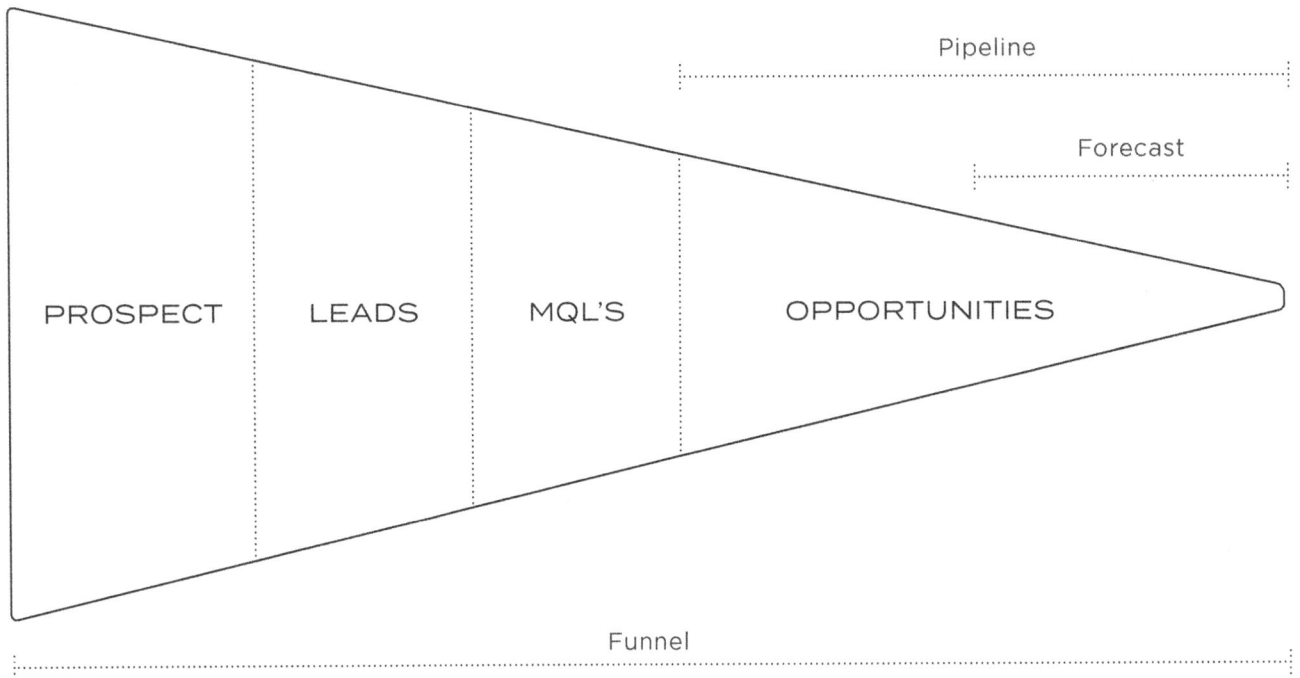

Pipeline

Forecast

PROSPECT   LEADS   MQL'S   OPPORTUNITIES

Funnel

Prospect – A potential customer that hasn't necessarily shown any interest in the company's offering yet

Lead – A potential customer that has shown interest

MQL – Marketing has qualified a lead and it is passed on to the sales department

Opportunities – Potential deals that have been converted to opportunities that an account executive starts working on

Many people say that funnel-thinking is dead, because the customer journey is so complex. But the fact is that buying at its core has not changed. The funnel model with its stages is a simplified stage-by-stage model of how customers mature from not having any needs, to becoming aware, then thinking, analyzing and finally at some point taking a decision. A great sales process is always aligned with the buying process, and the goal is to get customers interested and accelerate their buying process. The previous funnel graph should lead to more holistic thinking when developing the way that you market, sell and serve, instead of just thinking about opportunities in the sales pipeline. The role of marketing can be very strategic or tactical, or both.

In fast-growth companies marketing is usually very focused on creating demand in the market and growing the funnel for sales, while in more mature or stable phases of a company, marketing will also be focusing on growing current customers.

Next we'll look at four different ways of creating the necessary alignment between marketing and sales.

STEPS TO ALIGNING MARKETING AND SALES

1. Make sure marketing is result focused

The first problem with alignment is that sales has been accountable for revenue while marketing has not been as accountable for driving tangible results. It's hard to align two teams when they don't have shared goals and ways of producing results. Just like sales, the activity of marketing can be fully transparent now with the right systems and analytics in place. Marketing should be made accountable for delivering results. This is the first step towards aligning marketing and sales. An example of alignment and accountability could be that company X has a goal of increasing revenue by 50 million. They have budgeted that 30 million of the growth will come from current customers. The other $20 million will come from new customers. Marketing believes that with their current budget, they can produce leads worth about 15 million in new business. The numbers are calculated and with an additional investment, marketing agrees that it can produce enough leads to account for 20 million. Just like sales is budgeted, tracked and improved throughout the years, so too is marketing.

2. Put SLAs in place (service-level agreements)

Cooperation without rules and processes is very difficult, whether it is team sports or business we are talking about. That's why having a written service-level agreement about how sales and marketing will work together and what they are ready to commit to is key for successful cooperation. In its simplest form, an SLA is merely a document that says what marketing is willing to provide to sales, how, and vice versa. Sales makes a promise to handle leads at a certain speed and in a certain consistent way and marketing commits to qualifying them to a certain level and providing certain information about the leads when they are passed over to sales.

3. Create a joint language

Without a joint language it is hard to have a common understanding and cooperate efficiently. In many organizations there is not a consensus even on the most basic terms such as lead, prospect, MQL and SQL. In some companies a lead can mean to some sales executives just a list of random prospects, while to others a lead truly means a person who has shown interest in some way or another towards the company and its offering. Even though the joint language is written out and documented, this still does not mean that people will be using the terms correctly, so it is up to the managers and leaders to ensure that a common language is being used on all levels.

4. Create a sales and marketing blueprint

Think of your sales and marketing functions working together as an engine, with different parts that lock into each other and impact each other. A minor problem in one part of the engine can mean that you will have major problems in other parts.

A sales and marketing blueprint clearly shows what happens to a lead and where it comes from, who is responsible and what are the next steps. The blueprint should have an answer to how a potential customer goes from prospect to lead to a won opportunity in your systems and who is responsible by phase. A blueprint will tell you how everything fits nicely together.

With the blueprint you will be able to develop and trim your sales and marketing engine to its fullest potential.

Here is a sample of a sales and marketing blueprint from a lead generation point of view.

SIMPLIFIED LEAD TO OPPORTUNITY BLUEPRINT

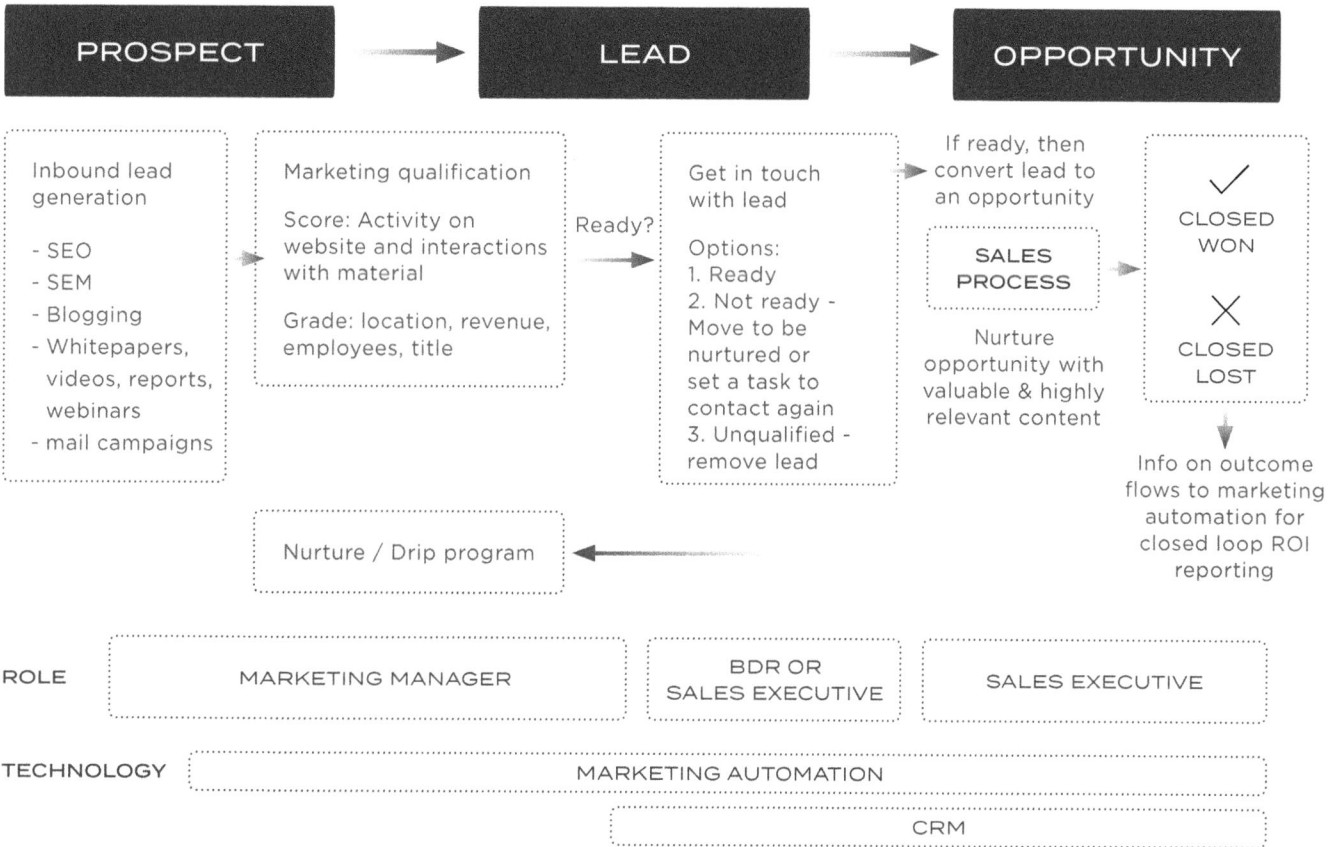

PROSPECT	→	LEAD	→	OPPORTUNITY

Inbound lead generation

- SEO
- SEM
- Blogging
- Whitepapers, videos, reports, webinars
- mail campaigns

Marketing qualification

Score: Activity on website and interactions with material

Grade: location, revenue, employees, title

Ready?

Get in touch with lead

Options:
1. Ready
2. Not ready - Move to be nurtured or set a task to contact again
3. Unqualified - remove lead

If ready, then convert lead to an opportunity

SALES PROCESS

Nurture opportunity with valuable & highly relevant content

✓ CLOSED WON

✗ CLOSED LOST

Info on outcome flows to marketing automation for closed loop ROI reporting

Nurture / Drip program

ROLE	MARKETING MANAGER	BDR OR SALES EXECUTIVE	SALES EXECUTIVE

TECHNOLOGY	MARKETING AUTOMATION

CRM

The negative side to lead generation is that many companies are generating a great number of leads and sometimes even too many for the sales team to handle, which often means there are a lot of low quality leads that sales executives get frustrated with.

Sales executives are already super busy, so the more qualified and nurtured a lead is the better. Depending on your business you may want a business development representative (BDR) qualifying leads and handing them over to account executives. The BDR is specifically trained to qualify and in most cases understand where the customer is in their buying process and what their reasons for buying are. It's much easier for the account executive to take over once the BDR has collected information about the customer and qualified the opportunity properly.

Do your best to nurture a lead for as long as possible without slowing down the buying process. If a sales executive would be able to speed up the buying process and close the deal, then it is clear that there is no need to nurture the prospect any longer. Perhaps in some segments you* can nurture right up until the point of sale, whereas an enterprise customer needs an account executive to jump in early on to diagnose and navigate.

CUSTOMER SUCCESS

Solutions get more complex as products, services and software are bundled together and at the same time customers have more options to choose from. The challenge for vendors is not only to get customers to buy or test out their products, but make sure that they fully use them and gain true business value, so that they will keep using the products in the long term, increasing the lifetime value. When companies invested in assets and signed off a contract before, the selling part was done, but now the race doesn't stop when the contract is signed. Customers can terminate their contracts, so they must be gaining the value they expected. It's like the contract is on the line every day. The vendor needs to be interested in making the customer happy, and it certainly pays off. Once a customer fully adopts a product, it creates a barrier to entry for competitors. Financially, it's also a win-win to improve customer retention. In 2013, Bain & Co. estimated that:

*"a 5% increase in customer retention rates can increase profits from 25% to 95%."**

* www.cmo.com/features/articles/2013/7/18/customer_retention.html

SO WHAT IS CUSTOMER SUCCESS ACTUALLY?

In an article by Drift, the chat solution company, they defined customer success in the following way:

"Unlike customer support, whose primary goal is to solve customer issues as they arise, customer success takes a longer-term view of the customer relationship. From day one, the mission of customer success is to help customers derive as much value from the product as possible."[*]

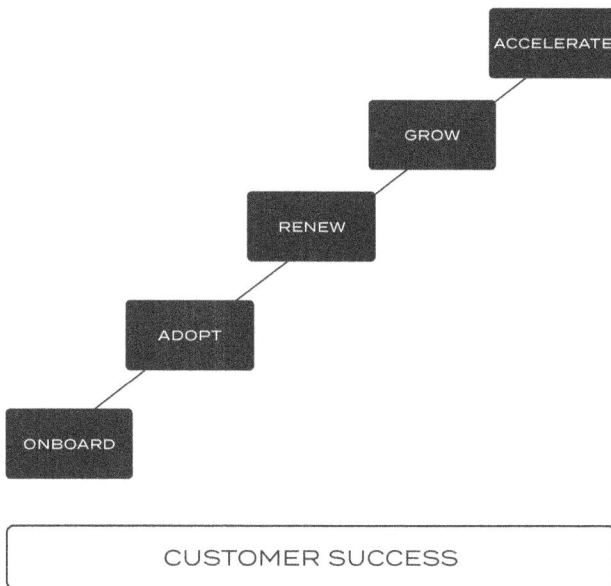

In general, customer support/service is more of a reactive team helping customers, while customer success is a proactive team that is strictly guided by KPIs for adoption and customer satisfaction. When customer success does a great job, customers get the value they originally planned or expected, which means that renewing contracts becomes easier and the potential for growing a customer to commit to a larger part of your portfolio of products and services increases. In some organizations customer success is also responsible for cross-selling and up-selling. The expertise of the customer success team does not necessarily have to be offered to all customers, but rather only premium customers.

We see customer success becoming more important in other industries, not just typical SaaS, because all companies are moving towards subscription- and outcome-based business models and therefore focusing on the long-term and customer-lifetime value.

With the help of analytics, customer success teams can see how customers are using products and services so that they can proactively step in if they see something alarming. Something alarming could be a type of behavior typically representing an unsatisfied customer. This could be, for example, a low level of product use, or clearly a low level of benefit or a lack of typical communications with the company.

ACCELERATE

GROW

RENEW

ADOPT

ONBOARD

CUSTOMER SUCCESS

THE CONNECTED PRODUCT IS A GAME CHANGER

Connected products create a bridge between the customers and your company. Connected products will make it easier to diagnose problems or take preventive measures before problems arise. A connected and intelligent product can also in itself be built around the principles of customer success. For example, a certain type of usage creates an automated message about how the customer could be benefitting from x and y add-ons. When the product is connected, it's not just the customer success team that personally helps customers gain business benefits; they also design and improve how the product (automatically) communicates with customers. Another example could be that customers who have a specific type of machine, and typically experience certain challenges, are recommended a bundle of spare parts and a certain service contract by means of automatic messaging. This is where artificial intelligence will be a big game changer.

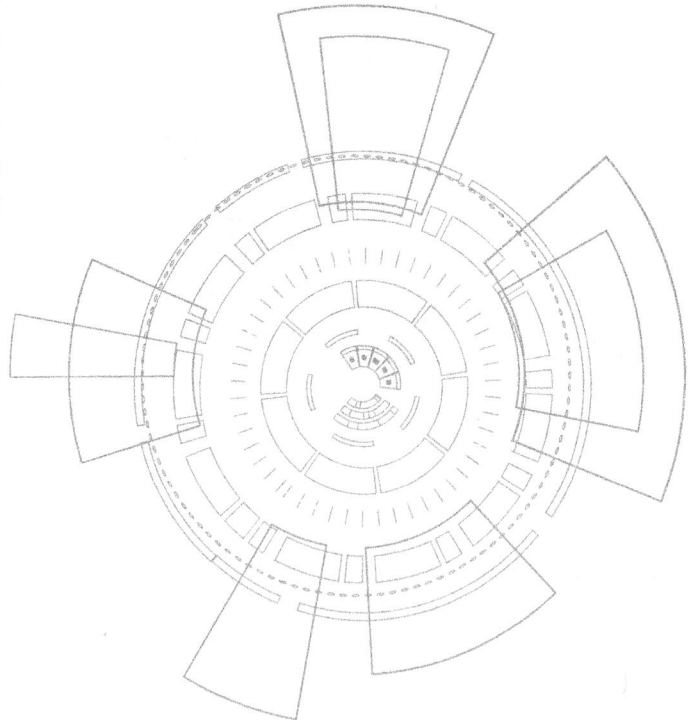

INTERVIEW: MARCO CLAZING, VP AND REGIONAL LEADER OF CUSTOMER SUCCESS GROUP EMEA NORTH AT SALESFORCE

LET'S START BY DEFINING CUSTOMER SUCCESS. WHAT IS IT ACTUALLY?

It is really joint success with the customer. Success can look very different if you look at it only from an individual's perspective. But when you define together with the customer what success looks like, you move away from a traditional customer-vendor relationship towards more of a partnership. So instead of looking only from your company's point of view, you define success according to your customer's business priorities, what's important to them and how you can help them reach those objectives. We have a framework for that with our customers which is called Compass. With Compass, we can align our customer targets with our targets so that it is a mutual roadmap to success.

YOU WORKED IN IT PROJECT SALES AND DELIVERY EARLIER. NOW THAT YOU ARE WORKING IN THE CONTINUOUS SUBSCRIPTION BUSINESS WORLD WHAT IS DIFFERENT?

It's actually the customer success model and how it's been ingrained within this company. I haven't seen any other company like that, starting with employee titles. We don't have HR we have Employee Success; they set up every employee for success. We are the company that had since the early days a person in charge of customer success, with the title Customer Success Manager. And now customers aren't seeing us like a software vendor but as a partner to help drive their digital transformation and drive innovation.

WHAT IS THE IMPORTANCE OF ONBOARDING AND HOW DO YOU ONBOARD CUSTOMERS?

If onboarding is not done right, then your product's adoption will be unsuccessful and in the end the customer will not see the value and they won't renew the contract.

We work tightly with our sales organization so that we know well ahead of time what types of customers and projects we are getting. This ensures that onboarding can be started right away when we get that new customer, and handovers are always timely and well managed. After onboarding we start providing the customer with resources and monitoring, for example, what kind of cases we are receiving from the customer or from their partner. Based on the evaluated need, we start educating the customer.

Our success organization consists of account partners, customer success management, advisory services, strategic projects and specialists. All of these roles help us understand the customer better throughout their journey so we can help them efficiently where needed.

The key metric we use is adoption and often the question is how do you measure adoption? We use something called Early Warning System (EWS), which consists of telling indicators of the customer's use of our services. We don't see their data, but we see how they benchmark against their peer group. EWS contains many sophisticated algorithms but one simple metric is, for example, how often the users are logging into the system. With that information we can interpret if the customer sees the value or not. And this login rate is one leading indicator for renewals; the higher the login rate, the better it is. If EWS is not looking good, it is a good time to discuss with the customer where the problem is and how we can help with that. Sometimes it's our Success Manager starting these discussions, sometimes it's the partner and many times it's the customer on their own.

WHAT IS YOUR ADVICE FOR BUSINESS LEADERS WHO WANT TO BUILD A CUSTOMER SUCCESS MODEL?

Many companies want to move in this direction, but to do so you need to put the customer into the center. As easy as it sounds, it's really hard and many companies don't know how to do that. We, for example, have a specific team that is only doing customer experience design and they help customers change their approach in their go-to market strategy, organization or in any other parts they have issues with. If we take, for example, a bank and its customer. The customer expects to receive the same service in each channel: they may want to chat online, then move to social media and then call the bank. Too often the banks internally have made organizational and technical barriers that prevent a unified experience for customers. Basically, there is lack of cooperation and single truth about that customer. The customer is in the worst case only a bank account number.

So, a customer-centric approach and design is a must. My personal example is from a discussion I had when I met with the CDO of a motor boat engine company. I have this engine, it costs quite a lot and this company doesn't even know who I am. I need to service it once a year, I need to find the right dealer who can do it and come to my boat as it's so big that I cannot move it. At some point I will also want to buy a new engine, or maybe a new propeller before that. But as they are not connected with me, for example via an app which would know where I am and when the engine was last serviced, they are missing plenty of opportunities to build a relationship and loyalty with me. It is not that difficult if the company has put the customer at the center of their development initiatives.

WHAT IS THE IDEAL FOCUS OF A CUSTOMER SUCCESS MANAGER?

We have debated lots about whether we should verticalize customer success and our services based on industry or products. My point is that our customers know their industry and business best but we need to help them drive innovation and transformation based on our platform and capabilities. The industry knowledge will certainly make it easier to talk the same language but understanding the key challenges and how to help with those is far more important.

HOW DO YOU USE TECHNOLOGY IN CUSTOMER SUCCESS MANAGEMENT?

We are already testing Artificial Intelligence in customer support, because it will allow us to scale what we are doing. We are growing so rapidly and it's not easy to find skilled people, so we need to understand how to help and drive the productivity of our employees in a positive way. For example, a very senior success manager should focus on things that they are best at, not on repetitive tasks. Certain things will be more suitable for technology platforms to handle than others. In our onboarding process, about 50% of tasks are handled by technology already. Bigger customers will receive high-touch success management and the long tail of smaller customers are on a more automated journey with webinars and so on. For these long-tail customers, we also have people taking care of their success, we call it customer success at scale. So, we aren't only helping our customers innovate, but we are helping them go through changes at maximum speed. We balance high touch, scale and automation by considering various factors, like complexity, size, and the products the customer is using. They all influence the model of customer success for a specific customer.

CHAPTER 11

/ TECHNOLOGY COMPONENTS OF YOUR GROWTH PLATFORM

You've most likely heard of the term, 'The Fourth Industrial Revolution' that we are now living in. This was a phrase first used in 2016 at the World Economic Forum that was also included in a book by Klaus Schwab.[*] We've arrived in the fourth industrial revolution through the first three revolutions, which were the steam and electricity revolutions, and the computing revolution. Now we are in an era where things and people are becoming connected to each other 24/7, physical and digital are blending together and artificial intelligence is becoming a part of everyday life. The fourth industrial revolution means we will get more data about our customers from products and services they have bought and how they use them, all enhanced by intelligence. The possibilities seem endless, but becoming advanced and reaching greater heights and being able to scale business for growth, means that companies need to master the basics and have the right fundamentals in place.

The practices covered in this book, such as sales and marketing alignment, customer success and taking control of the customer lifecycle, all become nearly impossible without the help of technology.

Technology is interesting, because although it enables so much and is a huge area of focus for many companies, by itself it still often solves nothing, without changing the operating model. At the same time, however, just adopting and using new technology for the sake of technology has, and will always be a bad idea. With a clear vision and strategy and alignment within your organization, defined customer processes and lifecycle phases, the right roles and skills of the organization, a technology project can succeed.

Our focus here is to open the different building blocks of the technology part of a Growth Platform. We could have left this chapter out maybe 20-30 years ago, and still have had a solid manual for B2B growth. We are, however, now at a point in time where technology and people and processes cannot be separated. Those not using and constantly adapting to technology will fall behind and become obsolete.

There are thousands of different applications that can be used in sales, marketing and service, but we will now focus on the key elements that need to be in place for a Growth Platform to function for a typical B2B company.

[*] en.wikipedia.org/wiki/Fourth_Industrial_Revolution

KEY PARTS OF THE TECHNOLOGY INFRASTRUCTURE

Enterprise Resource Planning (ERP) systems were the key focus of companies for a long time. Optimizing the supply chain created a competitive advantage in the product age, in the age when Walmart became a leader. These ERP systems were very rigid and hard to scale and integrate. But even though ERPs were and are rigid, they are still needed for business-critical things such as supply chain management, procurement, production, finance, payroll, and billing.

ERPs have been the essential business platforms, but are not by themselves sufficient for succeeding in this era of customer empowerment. In the late 90s CRMs started to become more widely adopted because of the realization that the supply chain was starting to work well enough and customer understanding and customer management would be the way to increasing growth and profits. The arrival of CRM in the 90s gave companies a 360-degree view of customers and the ability to steer the organizations towards their business goals. Since the first days of CRM, companies wanted open technology ecosystems, but technology vendors and technology integrators were not been able to deliver open technology, only proprietary technology. Nowadays, a CRM is not just an internal system, but an open system that customers and other stakeholders can use together with the customer.

But now ERP systems must still be in place, but the best practices and technology available have become commoditized. The next wave of competitive advantage – introduced in part two of this book – is customer experience and that is why CRMs are even more important now. Customer experience is managed with CRM systems, so we will refer to CRMs from this point onwards as 'systems of engagement'. A system of engagement comprises of all the different components of a CRM ecosystem. Systems of engagement are the foundation of success when it comes to customer lifecycle management. Systems of engagement are quite different from systems of record, aka ERPs. Systems of engagement – very broadly thought as nowadays as CRM consist of the following main parts:

- Marketing
- Sales
- Service
- Community & Commerce

ERPs give a good view of tangible business facts of that which has happened, while systems of engagement are the technology layer in the front office that gives a 360-view of customers and helps execute the daily business.

The term, CRM, should be thought of as much broader these days, now that customer relationship management is not just something sales executives are responsible for. Instead the customer relationship is now managed by several different roles within the organization, as we uncovered in Chapter 9 – Re-designing roles to support the customer journey.

Depending on the nature of your business, the roles of your systems of engagement will look very different. The roles of the different systems may also differ within one company depending on the customer segment that is being managed. Complex sales will have a large focus on a sales CRM, while a more commoditized product will have marketing automation and commerce, with service systems supporting. One thing that is common across all businesses is that relationships and personalization matters. Your technology infrastructure should help you create personalization and allow for nurturing relationships at scale. Whether automated or human touch, your messages to customers need to be as personalized as possible, and this is what the systems of engagement help do.

In the next graph you see the different systems of engagement and a sample of which customer lifecycle phases they would be used in.

TECHNOLOGY INFRASTRUCTURE OF YOUR GROWTH PLATFORM

The systems of engagement

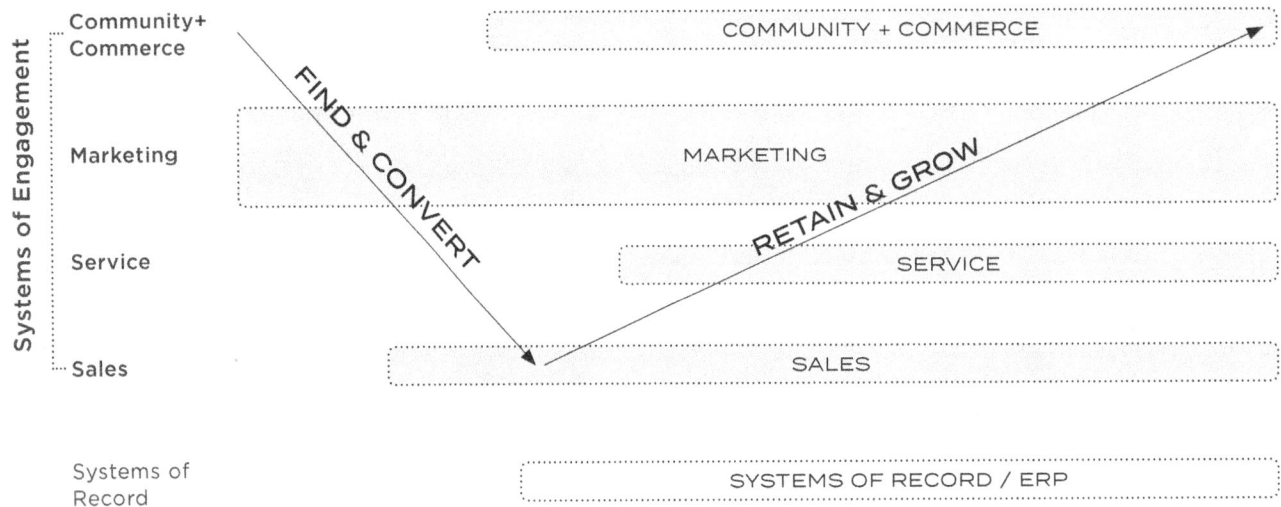

MARKETING TECHNOLOGY

In Chapter 4, we learned that buyers are 57% of the way through the buying process when they get in touch with sales[*] and it is the responsibility of sales executives to educate and consult customers. While sales people don't scale, marketing does. That is the key difference. Both should be educating and helping clients diagnose and figure out where they have problems. This is how marketing creates demand and it can be done at scale. Marketing is, however, not any longer just about creating demand and filling the funnel, but broader than that because marketing can directly drive revenue.

Marketing is generating revenue in three ways:

1. Indirectly, by generating leads, as well as cross-sell and up-sell opportunities that turn into revenue

2. Directly, by generating orders via e-commerce or portals.

3. Indirectly, by nurturing opportunities while an account executive is working on the opportunity

Since all of this requires a massive amount of content, there needs to be infrastructure to orchestrate pre-defined customers journeys both for campaigns and for certain marketing paths that are 'always on'. The marketing technology space has really blown up over the years, so an entire book could have been written about this topic alone, but here we'll mention some typical pieces of infrastructure in the marketing engagement layer.

Content management system/website – Your website and domains are your homes on the web to where you direct traffic. It's like the traditional storefront, but you can also have advertising and live promotion outside it.

Campaign management and landing pages – A central place for building and tracking campaigns. This capability would typically be found in most marketing automation platforms.

Customer journeys – Making all kinds of predefined content journeys that will help customers go forward in the buying process is a necessity for the modern marketer. This can either be used for nurturing leads or educating customers about specific challenges they may have. What makes journey building so powerful is that a marketer can decide exactly which type of customer behavior will launch specific marketing actions.

[*] www.cebglobal.com/marketing-communications/digital-evolution.html

Lead scoring and grading – When a website visitor downloads a piece of content they are requested to leave some type of information such as an email address. As they download another piece of content they will be requested to provide a new piece of information. Like this, information is traded between two parties and both get value out of it. In the background this website visitor can be given a profile, and based on what they are doing on the website and what content they are consuming, they will receive a score. The grade is based on the potential value of the customer and their level within the organization. This feature would typically be found in most marketing automation platforms.

Social media management – Customers are spending an increasing amount of time on social media, so it makes sense that social is a very important source of traffic and engagement with potential customers. Being active on Twitter, LinkedIn and Facebook means posting content and following up on comments throughout the whole day. This becomes very difficult to manage without a tool that helps coordinate and follow-up all social media activity.

Newsletter and email – A newsletter is something continuous that can bring value in the form of news or industry insights. You know you have a great newsletter if customers would even be willing to pay to be able to receive your newsletter. That should be something every marketer should

strive for; marketing so valuable that customers are willing to pay something for it! Sending newsletters and emails is already standard functionality in nearly all marketing tools, so don't get too hung up on the technology, but focus on the content and concept.

Web analytics – Web analytics tools like Google Analytics give a holistic view of website traffic, and how paid advertisements, content, SEO, SEM are working, and will help you fine tune your marketing. The very great thing now in marketing is that so much can be tracked, and you have a wealth of data, but the challenge is how to understand the data and know what data is actionable.

Marketing automation dashboards – When running several campaigns, and having 'always on' marketing paths, the only way to improve is to continuously monitor performance. Since B2B lead generation ROI can be measured by connecting leads with won opportunities, it is now much easier to measure ROI, since CRM systems have become widely used.

Dashboards could show things like leads created, by volume and revenue generated, pipeline created showing traffic sources, cost of customer acquisition and lead conversion rates. The dashboards help with what Niklas Sluijter of Smarp said they always strive for in their marketing, which is achieving results.

He said, *"At the end of the day it comes down to how much money we are spending and how much business we are getting with that money, so how much sales can close on what we bring them"*

SALES TECHNOLOGY

According to a fresh study, sales executives only spend 36% of their time selling.[*] This is just the time spent, without considering the quality of work. If we could increase both productivity and quality, we would be increasing their capability to perform.

The sales part of the engagement layer is the Sales CRM. Instead of using several systems, sales executives should only be working in one primary system that lets them do everything they need. At its best it is a one-stop shop from where sales executives can run their daily sales work, where they get a full view of all available customer information and also information that may be in other systems, like ERP.

Here are some typical features of the sales CRM.

Account and contacts management – Being able to see the hierarchies of organizations and who reports to whom, with a full history of accounts and contacts.

Opportunity management – Since B2B selling is typically about building a pipeline and closing deals, this opportunity management feature is the backbone of most CRMs. At its best the opportunity stages and functionality in the CRM help guide sales executives, but a standard CRM may not have this. At its worst a CRM can be a time-consuming reporting tool, designed for management to follow pipeline statistics and get their forecasts.

Lead management and campaigns – Tracking leads and converting qualified leads. Converting leads to opportunities, and tracking them towards won deals allows marketing and sales to constantly improve lead generation. Campaigns give full visibility into what marketing is doing, and which accounts and contacts are engaging with marketing content.

CPQ (Configure, price, quote tool) – CPQ helps streamline time-consuming and error-prone tasks, and ensures that sales people are guided throughout the process.

Collaboration within the CRM – Everything related to accounts, contacts and opportunities is critical information that lots of people need to know about often. If this information gets stuck in the inbox of a few people, or discussed face-to-face or over the phone or via online chat, then the 360-view of the customer will never be achieved. It is the continuous communication around accounts, contacts and opportunities that we want to have around the customers inside the CRM, so everyone is aligned and there is full transparency and trackability.

Integration with email and calendar – There is no reason that a sales executive should need to manually save emails or log meetings. Sales execs receive notifications when their e-mails are opened, and when someone engages with the content that they have sent.

Mobile application – Sales executives are on the go, from one place and one meeting to the next. Being able to use the CRM with ease and updating information is a must.

Dashboards – Everyone on all levels of the organization, from the executive team to sales personnel, have their own commercial KPIs that guide their work. These KPIs should be clearly visible and configurable in the CRM. Sales dashboards could show sales activity, created pipeline, average deal size, opportunity cycle, set target vs. monthly, quarterly or annual sales achieved.

Reports – Reports show many standard things, but reports can also be customized if there is something specific that a sales executive wants to see, like all the leads that converted last year from different trade fairs.

A key point here is that as sales executives no longer work alone. As a result, there are only minor benefits from sales executives using a CRM that is not connected or on the same platform as marketing and customer service/support or customer success. The CRM should be gluing the different people together, so there is one central place to view all customer data and work as intelligently as possible.

Increasingly, AI will be embedded and will be an assistant to sales people, guiding them and giving insight on things they may not have noticed or thought about. The more customers and opportunities a sales executive is working on, the more benefit they will get from AI. For example, a sales executive working in a SMB or mid-market segment in telecom or insurance will have multiple opportunities to work on every day, in contrast to someone selling one or two large deals per year.

SERVICE TECHNOLOGY

If you have a business model that puts you in a continuous relationship with customers, then your customers will pay for as long as they get enough value from the relationship. In this situation your service organization could be your biggest asset. The productivity of your service organization is crucial for business success.

To work productively, service agents need to have the same 360-visibility as sales people, so they can quickly solve issues for customers. They may even need to place orders for customers. When customers use critical machinery, for example, having an agreement in place for guaranteed support means that it is even more important to have excellent service technology. Everything needs to be tracked and managed, so that no matter who in the service organization is handling the customer, their problems will be solved in a timely fashion. And it's not just about taking care of issues efficiently, but also providing customers with a personalized experience. A personalized experience should be achievable even when different customer service representatives talk to the same customer.

In many companies, the goal of service is about increasing customer satisfaction and keeping customers happy, while also maintaining control or even decreasing services costs. Let's see what kind of customer service technology can help us achieve these goals.

Omnichannel customer service – The ability to continue a conversation with a customer across different channels such as email, SMS, website chat, phone, or social channels like Twitter and Facebook. While the service agent has one view of the conversation, the customer could be chatting through different channels, at different points in time.

Service console – To increase productivity, it helps to have a full view of the customer's history, including all interactions with sales executives, open customer cases, products ordered and products in use. While talking to a customer, this holistic view helps speed up support. This applies to different channels: online chat, telephone, community, social media.

Case management and prioritization – Being able to handle many cases and maintain high quality is a challenge. What can help is being able to prioritize which are low, medium, high or critical priority items. Without a system of prioritization and with many cases in the queue, it's hard to use the time of agents intelligently.

CTI integration – CTI stands for computer telephony integration, and it enables the telephone system and computers to be linked together. With CTI a service agent can see who is calling and view the most crucial information about the customer before answering the call. This improves the experience because the agent already knows more than the customer might expect.

Contracts, entitlements, assets/products in use – Having visibility about what the customer has bought and is using is a huge advantage. Sometimes the customer may not even be able to describe or remember the products they have. How are problems supposed to be solved by the agent in this case? Data from product usage will guide when and how to help customers, hopefully in an automated way. In this constantly connected world there is a wealth of data available on how the products you have sold are being used, so this data should not only help ensure customers are gaining all the benefits, but also new service innovations can be born from using customer data.

Routing – Sometimes solving problems becomes so complex that a certain type of experience is needed to solve them. In this situation it should be easy to route cases to the right people and track them with the help of the system.

Reports and dashboards – Following statistics like case resolution time and first response rate help develop the service organization.

Surveys – Surveys can give a deeper, more qualitative view of the service experience.

COMMUNITY AND COMMERCE TECHNOLOGY

Now that we are living in the age of the customer and social networks have gone online, wouldn't it make sense for companies to be there as well? Companies have an opportunity to join discussions and help facilitate them, and if trouble shows up there is a chance to react and help. Think if you could use the power of your happiest customers in a community to help you nurture your least happy customers early on to ensure they don't leave. The best companies are engaging with their customers and partners with the help of online communities and it's having a big impact on customer experience. An active community also makes it easier for your customer to purchase your products or service, if there is a high level of trust. For this reason, we have grouped commerce inside of the community part. When these two are syncing and armed with marketing automation, the setup becomes like the money printing machine that Niklas Sluijter talked about earlier.

A community is also something you can use to help channel partners grow their sales. Through the community you can share business opportunities to work on together or hand over to your partner. You can have a joint view of the business with the channel partner. Shared data and dashboards make it easier to develop the business together, instead of only working inside your own systems.

TYPICAL FEATURES OF A COMMUNITY

A community is a portal or online hub that you can use to communicate with customers. A community is not always going to be open for customers, but could as well be closed for the vendor and customer to have discussions. Think of it like internet banking, but with a greater experience. Customers can log in for added personalization. In the community, customers can find videos, articles and all kinds of valuable content. Do you want to be the one to provide this added-value content or are you going to let your competitors pull in your customers with their content?

There are really no limits to what you can have in your community; it all depends on the business requirements. For example, if there is a simple logic for how customers could order products, there is no reason why this simple process couldn't be included in the community.

One example of a community is what Wärtsilä, the provider of energy solution for marine and energy markets, has launched. They have a service for customers called Wärtsilä Online Services.* According to Wärtsilä, their solution enables customers to manage their installations and equipment efficiently by "accessing information whenever, wherever." The service includes things like "Technical Knowledge, Parts Online, TechRequest, Warranty Online, Field Services and a Maintenance planning tool."

For more complex commerce needs that do not make sense within a community, we'll have a look at commerce technology to discover the functionality that is required.

COMMERCE

If you have used Amazon, you know what a great experience can be like. Fast ordering, one-click purchasing, and a helpful recommendation engine. Many B2B web shops are far from this, even though the benefits could be very big for their business. A proper e-commerce solution could help provide products and solutions to customers who are unreachable now. The commerce solution could help expand the business by testing new markets that you cannot reach today with current resources.

For products that are easy to set-up and not risky to buy, it makes perfect sense to allow customers to self-order through an e-commerce platform. If browsing through the products and ordering is made easy for simple products, then the need for talking to an expert or sales rep is really not necessary from the customers perspective. Sales can spend time doing more valuable things than placing orders and customers can order faster. Its a win-win.

In B2B, it is the transparency of pricing that is a bit scary for many. As a result, a highly personalized buying experience has been the key competitive advantage for many companies that haven't been able to differentiate with their products or services. Luckily, solutions are developing very fast to improve the B2B buying experience. According to research firm Gartner, in 2018 around 40% of B2B commerce sites will be using price optimization algorithms to deliver dynamic pricing.* A more personalized approach will create more opportunities to benefit from e-commerce.

Typical features are: order management, order status and tracking, offers and subscription management, product catalogue management, contract/customer-specific pricing, click-to-chat, multi-currency and multi-language and different purchasing methods like credit card, invoice, PO, or the capability to set up accounts for different buyers with purchasing limits. These are just some features that make up a commerce solution.

The community and commerce solution need to be connected to sales, service and marketing solutions, so all the people interacting with customers have access to orders customers have placed and what they have in their shopping cart.

This commerce piece really sits together with Chapter 6, which was about the importance of segmenting. Even though e-commerce is a technical solution, implementing it is always a business transformation and not just another storefront or channel being put up, quite the opposite actually, because it impacts everything you do with your different customer segments.

POINT SOLUTIONS VS. ECOSYSTEMS

It is becoming more important to choose ecosystems and platforms for strategic business needs, rather than point solutions for every small specific business need. A point solution is a system that often solves a specific business problem, but contains the risk of not fitting in with the overall needs of the business. In the short term, putting a point solution in place will most likely be good for achieving the required impact, but in the longer term these point solutions won't scale and aren't always easy to integrate. You become a prisoner of your old decisions in developing the business.

The problems with point solutions could be that even changing a little field in one system, could mean that you need a separate IT project just to get that field changed in the other system linked to it. For example, a separate marketing automation system that is not well integrated with a CRM will become a mess if it creates duplicates or does not sync properly. Customers are also expecting real-time service, and if you are using different solutions, you must make sure every employee

 * www.insideretail.com.au/wp-content/uploads/2016/11/ analyst-report-critical-capabilities-for-digital-commerce-2016-en.pdf

and message sent to customers is based on real-time information from all systems that have customer-critical information.

For these reasons you should choose the ecosystem that is the best for your business looking holistically at the entire business's needs, not just the needs of one department or team.

IMPLEMENTING TECHNOLOGY

Whatever technology you are implementing, whether it be marketing, sales, service or community/commerce, keep your customer and your strategy at the center of your thinking. Your customer should be unified and visible across all the key technology components in your platform. The data model and account hierarchy shouldn't be different, even if you are using different technology parts from different vendors. Of course, it is easier if one technology vendor can offer a solution that scales across marketing, sales, service and community/commerce.

Before implementing technology, there needs to be a crystal-clear picture of where the company wants to go and how success will be defined and measured. This makes it easy to compare the current situation with where the company needs to go, so that the gap is clearly identified. They key question is: how do we need to change to reach our goal? Most often the technology is just a small part of the equation. As Kim Metcalf-Kupres

pointed out in our interview with her, it's wise to start with the end goal in mind and work your way back from there. Often, we see excited business leaders jumping on a trend or choosing a technology just because another company did it without going through the necessary evaluation of what they need. Solving business problems just with technology is most likely one part of the reason that so many digital transformation projects fail. According to Forbes, 84% of digital transformation projects fail.[*]

Here are the simplified steps needed to ensure that technology is implemented correctly.

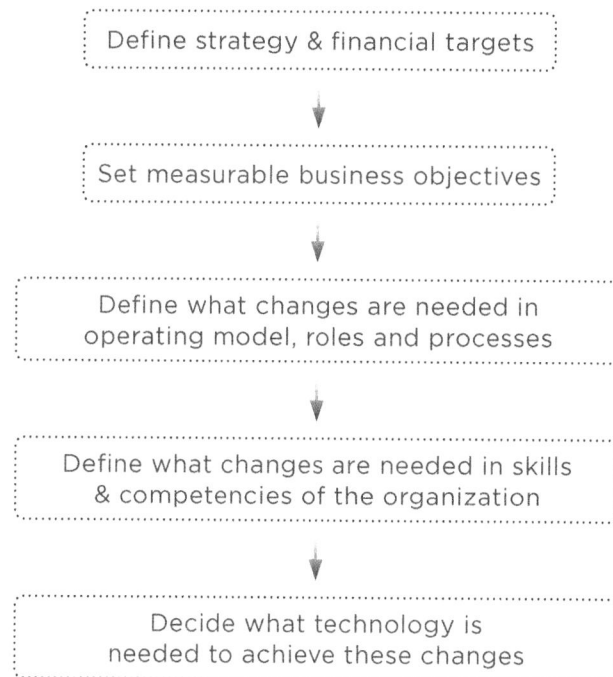

```
┌──────────────────────────────────────┐
│   Define strategy & financial targets │
└──────────────────────────────────────┘
                  ↓
┌──────────────────────────────────────┐
│   Set measurable business objectives  │
└──────────────────────────────────────┘
                  ↓
┌──────────────────────────────────────┐
│   Define what changes are needed in   │
│   operating model, roles and processes│
└──────────────────────────────────────┘
                  ↓
┌──────────────────────────────────────┐
│  Define what changes are needed in skills │
│   & competencies of the organization  │
└──────────────────────────────────────┘
                  ↓
┌──────────────────────────────────────┐
│     Decide what technology is         │
│   needed to achieve these changes     │
└──────────────────────────────────────┘
```

[*] www.forbes.com/sites/brucerogers/2016/01/07/why-84-of-companies-fail-at-digital-transformation/2/#999f64231931

APPROACHES TO AUTOMATING SPECIFIC PROCESSES

The starting point for thinking about automation is to understand the current situation and what kind of results need to be achieved. A few areas that are often automated first are the lead funnel and order management.

For marketing, automating the lead funnel could mean lead qualification with bots, or lead scoring and grading with the help of marketing automation so you know when someone should be contacted personally. Lead scoring refers to the activity level of someone on your site. A visitor earns a score by getting points based on how valuable the different parts of the website are that they have visited. Grade refers to the quality of the lead, which is defined by criteria such as the size of the company and the title of the person.

SEGMENT-BASED AUTOMATION APPROACH

Instead of deciding in general which processes or parts of the customer management model that could be automated, a segment-based approach may be the best way forward. Choose the segments that are the easiest to start with, for example C-level customers or those in tier 3, as some may call them.

Automating certain processes for C-level customers could be initiatives like automated renewals, or marketing automation campaigns for new products that would typically be done by phone.

Here are a few additional ideas for automation:

- Self-service customer service or bot assisted

- Order taking via e-commerce, instead of back-office taking orders

- Marketing automation for continuous messaging and staying top of mind with existing customers

- Instead of only outbound prospecting done by sales people, make sure a certain number of leads are constantly flowing with the help of marketing automation

NEW EMERGING TECHNOLOGIES

It is important to constantly be testing and evaluating new technologies, and seeing where it would make sense to be used on a larger scale (in the near future), even if the technology doesn't fully work today or isn't a wise economic decision today. Consider these as innovation experiments. The key is to not do too many at the same time, and make sure these tests are fully aligned with your strategic initiatives.

The companies that can choose which technologies to focus on and pick the right ones are building a competitive advantage and operating model that their competitors will be scrambling to catch up on later. Continuous goal-oriented testing will create a competitive advantage. This is the same thing that happened with e-commerce. It didn't fully explode at once, and the internet bubble bursting was a good example of this because the expectations and results did not match. The companies that have been building their operating model and capabilities to execute on e-commerce have been doing this for 20 years, slowly but surely creating a working model. It didn't happen overnight, but their vision has become a reality as e-commerce is mainstream now. The companies that weren't willing to innovate early, are now playing catch up.

Testing and tweaking your technology infrastructure should be continuous. The beauty of building a platform, where everything is tied nicely together, is that even small changes to your platform can have a big impact on how people in different parts or levels of the organization work. A minor addition to how a sales executive's activity is automatically tracked can potentially have a major impact on how marketing crafts and targets their messaging to customers, or how well customer support can help customers.

In this section we'll highlight a few interesting technologies that many are already gaining major business benefits from.

BOTS ARE NOW AUGMENTING OPTIMAL HUMAN BEHAVIOR

From the first website visit to a face-to-face meeting there could be several touchpoints with a customer. For example, a bot could help the customer with simple tasks through website chat or in social media.

Typical questions from customers are easy for bots to answer, for example:

"Where can I find information about product X"
"What is your pricing for product X"
"What are your opening hours for dealers in area X"

When the customer lands on the webpage, the bot lets the visitor know that it's a bot when the conversation starts. This is a lot better than figuring out later that the customer has been talking to a bot, thinking all along it was a human. This would make the customer feel tricked. The bot then asks how it can help and gives different options that the customer can choose from. Based on the answers, the bot could help assess what the customer's needs are and give a simple answer to what product or service matches the customer's needs. Alternatively, the bot can point the customer in the right direction to some reference cases. The bot could have access to multiple databases, calendars and email giving it even more power to take care of normal tasks done by humans, such as scheduling meetings.

As the bot talks to the customer it will be capturing important information that will make it much easier for a human to take over the conversation if needed. There is no reason why the bot couldn't make the deal and send the order confirmation to the customer.

Increasing the productivity of people is done by prioritizing what humans and what technology will support. Just like dogs are a part of a family, bots and automated messaging should be fully integrated as an important team member.

BOTS ARE DEVELOPING VERY FAST

According to inventor and futurist, Ray Kurzweil, chat bots will be indistinguishable from human chat conversations by the year 2029.[*] If this will hold true then the opportunities are enormous. We may not however, have to wait until 2029 because for example Google has already shown how their virtual assistant can make phone calls using natural speech. Demonstrations of this technology have already been shown in 2018 by Google, with technology they call Google Duplex.[**]

Many of the tasks that marketing, sales and service people do now are so repetitive and manual that there is definitely an opportunity to use bots in many parts of the customer journey. This is reality already for many companies and we do not believe that there are any companies that couldn't benefit from bots, especially from the perspective of the needs of marketing, sales and service.

When bots become team members, data management becomes more important. Bots will be able to use customer data to serve every customer, but they will not be able to think on the fly like humans do and improvise. They need data to be able to do more advanced things.

One big advantage of bots is that they are available 24/7 and they can remember everything. Here are a few things a bot can assist with:

- Steer website visitors to what they are looking for

- Proactively turn website visitors into qualified leads

- Book meetings

- Help customers diagnose their needs and propose products (also referred to as selling)

- Channel visitors to talk to the right person or department

ARTIFICIAL INTELLIGENCE USE CASES IN SALES AND MARKETING

As consumers, we interact with artificial intelligence constantly, but working within B2B as sales and marketing professionals, it hasn't fully been blended into our everyday lives yet. Slowly but surely, it's creeping up and being used by organizations that want to gain a competitive advantage by automating and making their workforce more efficient.

[*] www.theverge.com/2016/5/27/11801108/ray-kurzweil-building-chatbot-for-google
[**] www.theguardian.com/technology/2018/may/08/google-duplex-assistant-phone-calls-robot-human

Accenture mentions the following in one of their reports:

"The impact of AI technologies on business is projected to increase labor productivity by up to 40% and enable people to make more efficient use of their time."[*]

If the impact is projected to be this big, then it shouldn't be surprising that 72% of business leaders believe AI is going to create a business advantage, according to a PWC study.[**]

Let's put the future aside for a moment, and look at examples of how AI can already be used in sales and marketing today.

Opportunity probability – Traditionally, the seller decides on the probability of winning a deal or the probability is already defined in the opportunity stages. Artificial Intelligence can give its own point of view on what the probability is based on all the historical data it has available. AI will also tell you what types of actions will increase or decrease the chances of winning that opportunity.

Lead scoring – Based on historical information, artificial intelligence can be used to more accurately score what kind of leads will close and which will not and why.

Opportunity close date – Artificial intelligence can predict the date for an opportunity to close. For example, the seller may estimate that a deal will be won on June 15th, but artificial intelligence may predict that the more likely date for closing will be August 15th. AI will tell you why it estimates an additional 60 days will be needed and what actions could be taken to speed up the process. It's up to the sales executive to validate whether these are viable options.

ARTIFICIAL INTELLIGENCE IN SERVICE

The human brain is only capable of handling a certain workload and is not designed to multi-task and handle a high volume of work at once. While (some) humans are great at understanding another person, and generally much better at understanding the context of what the customer is saying, there is a great amount of data that can be used to enhance the customer's experience whether talking to a person, bot, or in a portal that provides a customized experience. Artificial intelligence is ripe for customer service and success, because of the amount of data there is available. Customer service seems like a natural place to start reaping the benefits of AI, because often customer service agents are creating more data than sales people, because the nature of work is somewhat different.

[*] www.accenture.com/sk-en/insight-artificial-intelligence-future-growth
[**] www.pwc.com/CISAI?WT.mc_id=CT1-PL52-DM2-TR1-LS4-ND6-BPA1-CN_CIS-AI-AIsocial

During our chat with Marco Clazing from Salesforce, we also discussed the role of AI and field service, which turned out to be an interesting discussion. Here is an example that came up during that discussion:

"Out of the trends going on right now, I believe AI will be the most important of them all. There are so many different things I could tell you about AI, but something that comes first to mind is for example our customer KONE where IBM's Watson is monitoring their elevators and seeing if something is taking for example 0.2 seconds longer than typical. Based on this measurement and how frequently it will happen the AI can estimate need of service. In this KONE example our field service solution is then optimizing preventive maintenance schedules and routes of the technicians so that they will handle their territory with the best productivity and the right priority of customer importance."

AUGMENTED AND VIRTUAL REALITY

There are many interesting technologies in addition to AI that are going to be supporting humans in their work, such as augmented reality (AR) and virtual reality (VR). Things will become much easier to achieve remotely or will be done without an expert on site. As a result, a machine could be fixed by someone who is not an expert. This person could be assisted by augmented reality, or virtually by a remote expert. So total amateurs could be fixing machines or performing work at the same level as a seasoned expert. These technologies haven't starting to bloom until now, even though they've been talked about for a really long time. As computing power, user interfaces, and voice and visual technology improves, it will make the use of these technologies spread much faster.

From a personal selling and customer service perspective, helping customers will become increasingly time and place irrelevant. This will increase the necessity for a technology infrastructure to support the organization and the different people who are working with customers.

WRAPPING UP THIS CHAPTER

In part two of this book we walked through the different stages of the customer lifecycle. In part three we defined what the organizations' roles and processes should look like, when built around the customer lifecycle. Without the technology covered in this chapter, the way a modern organization needs to work with its diverse roles would not be possible. Technology is very important; it is an enabler. Although it is tempting, the trick is to not get too excited about technology and develop anything for the sake of technology, but ensure it is present in all development initiatives. Now you have gotten a glimpse of each part of a Growth Platform.

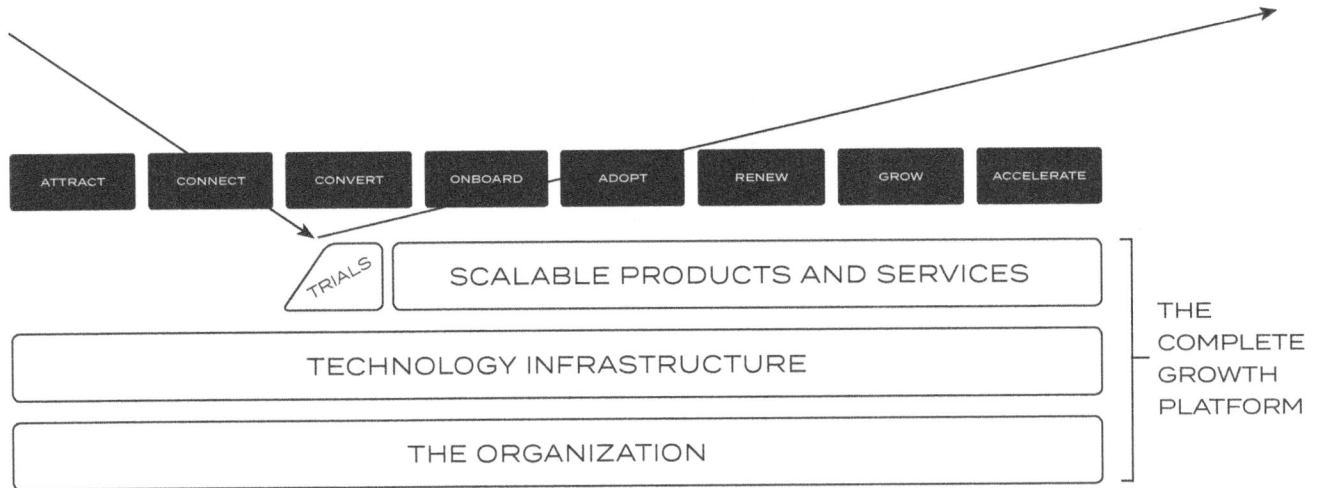

| ATTRACT | CONNECT | CONVERT | ONBOARD | ADOPT | RENEW | GROW | ACCELERATE |

TRIALS

SCALABLE PRODUCTS AND SERVICES

TECHNOLOGY INFRASTRUCTURE

THE ORGANIZATION

THE COMPLETE GROWTH PLATFORM

CHAPTER 12

/ WORKSHOP MATERIALS

In this chapter you will find one holistic canvas called the Action plan, which is a summary of the main themes in this book. Use it to collect thoughts and development ideas.

Before the Action plan canvas there are five more detailed canvas tools to help you dive more deeply into these areas:

1. Products/services/subscriptions revenue and profit analysis – This is called the Offering analysis

2. Customer segmentation analysis

3. Lifecycle stage analysis

4. Roles analysis

5. Technology analysis

Each canvas is used for a specific customer segment after which they are analyzed and compared to each other, so that it's easier to understand how the development needs differ between customer segments.

We have used these in workshops and you can do the same.

Available for download at www.axend.fi/revenuegrowthplatform

REVENUE

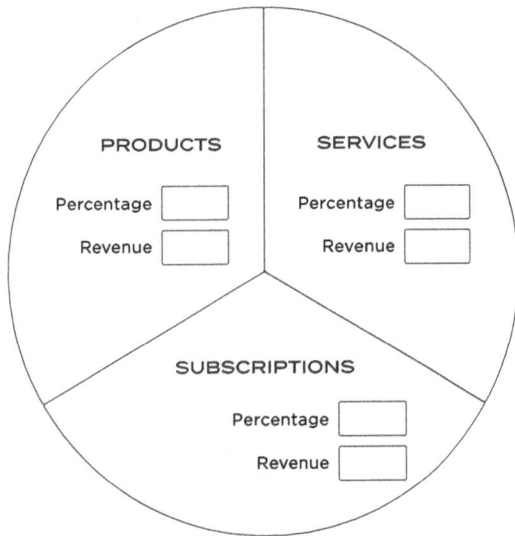

PROFIT

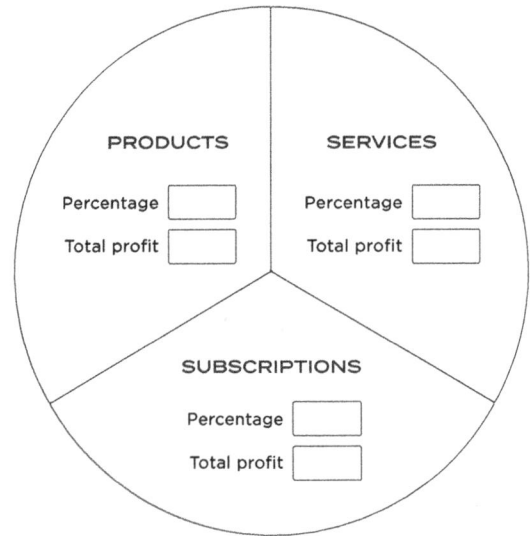

OBSERVATIONS:

ANNUAL ORDER VALUE

SEGMENT NAME

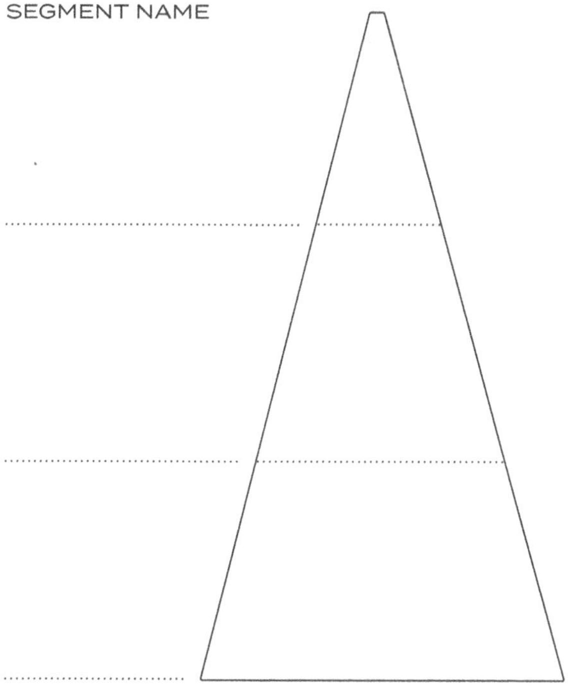

What is our goal with this segment?
What needs to change?
What type of investments need to be made?

How meny customers in this segment?

Average annual order value

WORKSHOP MATERIALS
/**LIFECYCLE STAGE ANALYSIS**

FIND & CONVERT

RETAIN & GROW

ATTRACT	CONNECT	CONVERT	ONBOARD	ADOPT	RENEW	GROW	ACCELERATE
What works?							
What needs improvement							

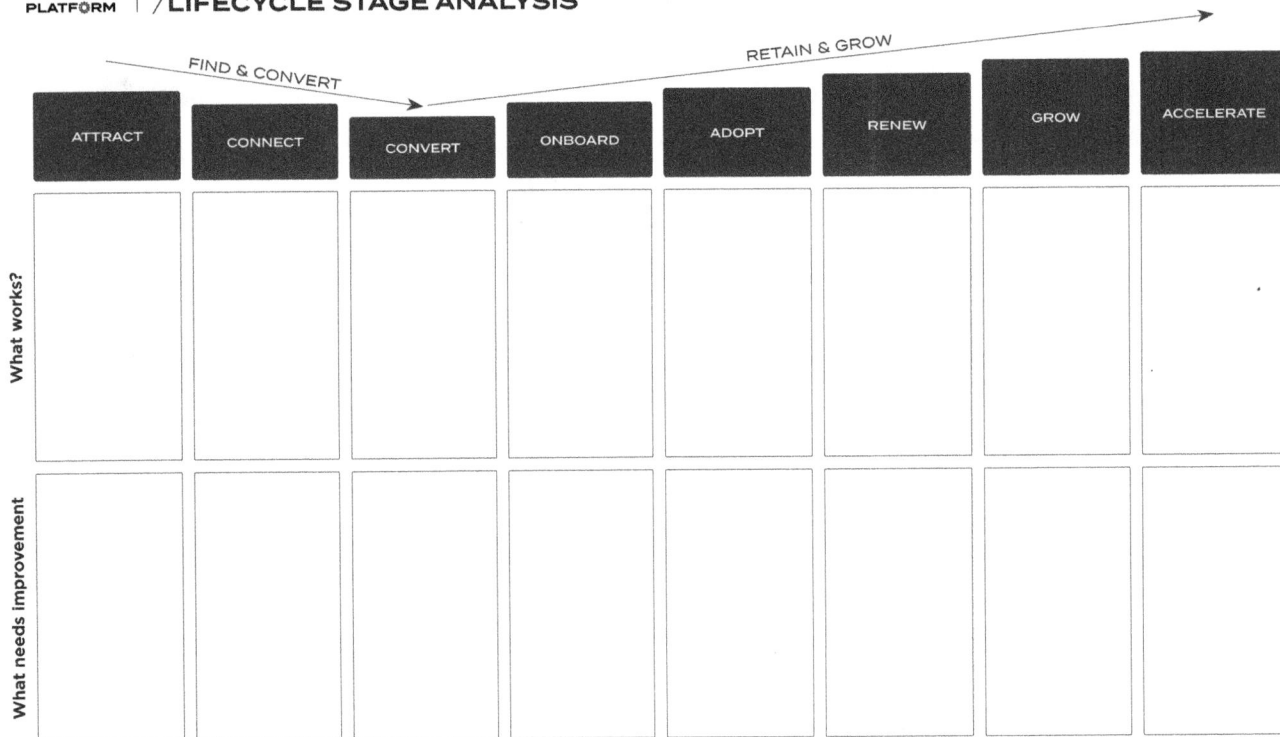

CUSTOMER SEGMENT: _____

REVENUE GROWTH PLATFORM | WORKSHOP MATERIALS
/ROLES ANALYSIS

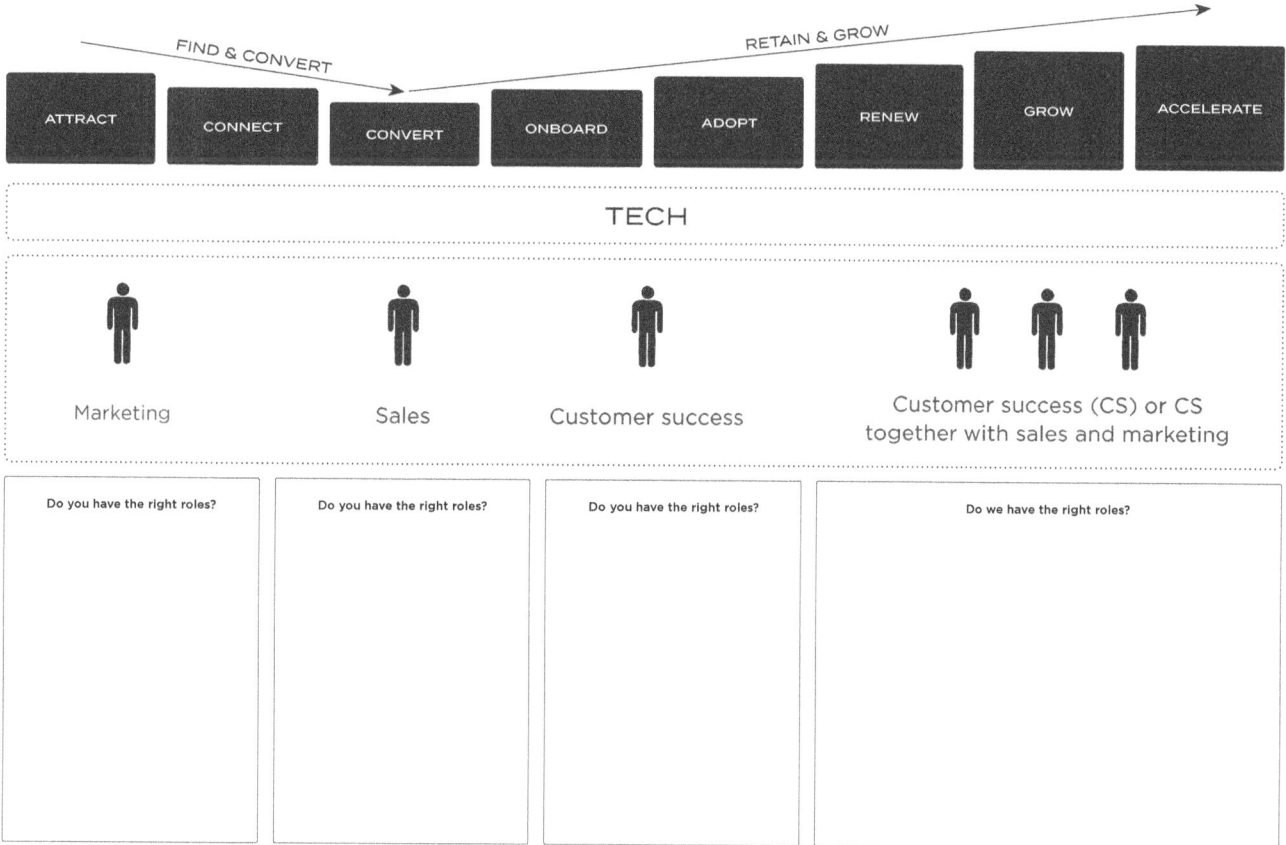

FIND & CONVERT

RETAIN & GROW

| ATTRACT | CONNECT | CONVERT | ONBOARD | ADOPT | RENEW | GROW | ACCELERATE |

TECH

Marketing

Sales

Customer success

Customer success (CS) or CS together with sales and marketing

Do you have the right roles?

Do you have the right roles?

Do you have the right roles?

Do we have the right roles?

WORKSHOP MATERIALS
/TECHNOLOGY ANALYSIS

FIND & CONVERT

RETAIN & GROW

CUSTOMER LIFECYCLE STAGES	ATTRACT	CONNECT	CONVERT	ONBOARD	ADOPT	RENEW	GROW	ACCELERATE
Community + Commerce								
Marketing								
Service								
Sales								

OFFERING

What were your key findings?
What needs to change?

SEGMENTS

What were your key findings?
What needs to change?

LIFECYCLE

What were your key findings?
What needs to change?

TECHNOLOGY

What were your key findings?
What needs to change?

ROLES

What were your key findings?
What needs to change?

ACKNOWLEDGEMENTS

Some have inspired us with their words to write this book, and others have inspired us with their actions. We want to thank the friends, family and customers who gave us words of encouragement along the way to keep this project going. Extra thanks go out to two special ladies who had the patience when nights and weekends were spent working on this project. Thank you Hanna and Heta.

This book would not have been possible without the people we had a chance to interview and talk with in the past 18 months. We want to give a special thanks to those we interviewed: Jaakko Paalanen, Niklas Sluijter, Mikko Leinonen, John Phillips, Marco Clazing, Simon Talling-Smith and Kim Metcalf-Kupres; your points of view and practical application of best practices gave depth and wisdom to the book.

Thank you to all the people who contributed to the project with their ideas or took time out of their busy schedules to read through the first drafts of this book. Thank you Juha Harju, Mikko Seppä, Ikla Puustinen, Kai Mäkelä, Petri Vilpponen, Aamer Hasu, Markus Salo, Fredrik Teir and Petteri Poutiainen.

Big thanks also to the team who made this book possible: Paul McNamara, Peter Seenan and Mikko Johansson.

ABOUT THE AUTHORS

Jan Ropponen helps B2B companies grow in highly competitive markets. Jan advises and trains both sales management and sales executives on topics such as modern sales processes and methodologies, as well as opportunity management. In previous roles Jan has worked both in management and sales positions in companies with services that cover CRM and marketing automation technologies, as well as digital marketing services.

For inquiries about speaking engagements, interviews or cooperation opportunities please contact via e-mail: jan.ropponen@axend.fi

Sami Lampinen works at Salesforce as VP of Sales and has nearly 20 years of experience in the CRM domain. He started working at Salesforce in 2007 and before that worked at Accenture in various roles. In the roles of CRM consultant, sales engineer and account executive, Sami has advised various enterprises on their transformations within sales, marketing, and service so that companies can become more agile and profitable. He's been "greasing their chains" as Sami would describe it himself.

Sami can be reached at lampinen@gmail.com

ABBREVIATIONS / TERMINOLOGY

API – Application programming interface. Makes it possible to connect systems so information flows from one system to another

ARR – Annual recurring revenue

B2B – Business to business sales

CAC – Customer acquisition cost

CAPEX – Capital expenditure are funds used by a company to acquire, upgrade, and maintain physical assets such as property, industrial buildings, or equipment. CAPEX is often used to undertake new projects or investments by the firm.

CLV – Customer lifetime value

CMO – Chief Marketing Officer

CPQ – Configure, price, quote tool

CRM – Customer relationship management system

CSO – Chief Sales Officer

CTR – Click-through rate (online advertising)

ERP – Enterprise resource planning system

IoT – Internet of things

KPI – Key performance indicator

Lead – A potential customer that has shown interest

MQL – Marketing qualified lead

MRR – Monthly recurring revenue

OPEX – Operating expenses are the costs for a company to run its business operations daily.

Opportunity – a qualified potential deal

Outcome based business model – Instead of buying a product or service, a customer buys a specified outcome that they benefit from directly.

Prospect – a potential client that fits an ideal customer profile, but that has not shown interested yet.

SEM – Search engine marketing

SEO – Search engine optimization

SQL – Sales qualified lead